Digital Competence Development in Higher Education

FOREIGN LANGUAGE TEACHING IN EUROPE

Edited by
Manuel Jiménez Raya, Terry Lamb and Flávia Viera

VOL. 12

Zu Qualitätssicherung und Peer Review der vorliegenden Publikation

Die Qualität der in dieser Reihe erscheinenden Arbeiten wird vor der Publikation durch Herausgeber der Reihe im Blind-Verfahren geprüft. Dabei ist der Autor der Arbeit den Gutachtern während der Prüfung namentlich nicht bekannt.

Notes on the quality assurance and peer review of this publication

Prior to publication, the quality of the work published in this series is blind reviewed by editors of the series. The referees are not aware of the author's name when performing their review.

María Luisa Pérez Cañado /
Juan Ráez Padilla (eds.)

Digital Competence Development in Higher Education

An International Perspective

PETER LANG
EDITION

Bibliographic Information published by the Deutsche Nationalbibliothek
The Deutsche Nationalbibliothek lists this publication in the Deutsche Nationalbibliografie; detailed bibliographic data is available in the internet at http://dnb.d-nb.de.

Library of Congress Cataloging-in-Publication Data
Digital competence development in higher education : an international perspective / María Luisa Pérez Cañado ; Juan Ráez Padilla (eds.) -- Peter Lang Edition.
pages cm -- (Foreign Language Teaching in Europe; Vol. 12)
ISBN 978-3-631-63803-3 -- ISBN 978-3-653-04536-9 (E-Book) 1. Language and languages--Study and teaching (Higher)--European Union countries. 2. Language and languages--Study and teaching (Higher)--Technological innovations--European Union countries. 3. Digital media--Social aspects--European Union countries. 4. Competency-based education--European Union countries. 5. Media programs (Education)--European Union countries. 6. Education, Higher--European Union countries. I. Pérez Cañado, María Luisa, editor. II. Ráez Padilla, Juan, editor.
P57.E9D54 2014
418.0071'14--dc23
2014023765

ISSN 1437-3157
ISBN 978-3-631-63803-3 (Print)
E-ISBN 978-3-653-04536-9 (E-Book)
DOI 10.3726/978-3-653-04536-9

Peter Lang Edition is an Imprint of Peter Lang GmbH.

Peter Lang – Frankfurt am Main · Bern · Bruxelles · New York · Oxford · Warszawa · Wien

This publication has been peer reviewed.

www.peterlang.com

Table of Contents

Introduction and Overview

María Luisa Pérez-Cañado & Juan Ráez-Padilla

The creation of the European Higher Education Area (EHEA) has deeply impacted tertiary education across the continent at all curricular and organizational levels. Objectives are now formulated in terms of learning outcomes, methodologies are becoming more student-centered, groupings and learning modalities are increasingly diversified, teacher and learner roles are being reconfigured, and assessment is more authentic, formative, and criterion-referenced (Pérez Cañado, 2010). Within didactic materials and resources, Information and Communication Technologies (ICTs) are now acquiring a particularly sharp relief.

Indeed, in addition to being one the core generic competencies which most European universities have worked into all their Bologna-adapted degrees, the potential of technological or digital competence for enhancing the student-centered learning process has been underscored in the official EHEA literature. According to Benito & Cruz (2007: 104), ICT is not a new fad, but a crucial tool which, in combination with the EHEA, will foster pedagogical innovation and allow all the agents involved in the teaching-learning process to expedite knowledge-building and competency development. Much the same is claimed by Pennock-Speck (2008: 70):

> ICT in the field of education is an exciting opportunity for teachers and students. With more and more teachers being expected to apply more student-centred teaching, even if they do not particularly want to (Bailey, 2008), practically all teachers will end up using ICT to teach or at least to communicate with or evaluate students to a greater or lesser extent.

The use of ICT for language learning or Computer Assisted Language Learning (CALL), perhaps the most widespread and acknowledged term, has developed particularly rapidly in recent years, coming to involve an increasingly diverse range of options relating to the principled application of new technologies in language learning. During the last three decades, CALL has progressed and evolved at a remarkable rate. Books are regularly published on the subject and at least four international journals are now dedicated to the topic. There are annual conferences devoted to it in many parts of the world, and highly active online discussion lists (Levy & Stockwell, 2006: 1).

Beatty (2003: 7) defines CALL as "any process in which a learner uses a computer and, as a result, improves his or her language" and considers it an "amorphous or unstructured discipline, constantly evolving both in terms of pedagogy and technological advances in hardware and software" (2003: 8). Sure enough, as Beatty (2003), Lee (2000), Levy (1997), Pérez Gutiérrez & Pérez Torres (2005), or Warschauer & Healey (1998) document, CALL has undergone three main phases, with each stage corresponding to a different level of technology and certain pedagogical theories.

Behaviorist CALL was conceived in the 1950s and implemented in the next two decades. As it name indicates, it was based on the behaviorist learning model underlying Audiolingualism and thus featured repetitive language drills, explicit grammar and vocabulary instruction, and activities focused on form. The latter were corrected by the computer, which fulfilled the role of mechanical tutor.

Communicative CALL emerged in the 1980s as a reaction to the behaviorist view of language teaching. It was based on cognitive theories which saw learning as a creative process of discovery and thus incorporated more interactive and varied programs. Computers were employed for conducting individual work and popular CALL software involved reconstruction, concordancing, and simulations.

Finally, integrative CALL has superseded the previous two types of CALL from the 1990s onwards. With its underlying socio-cognitive view and consequent emphasis on real language use in a meaningful, authentic context, it is based on skills integration, multimedia-networked computers, and the Internet, and employs varied and hybrid CALL programs, where the computer acts as tutor, stimulus, and tool. The evolution of CALL can be visually traced in the summary provided in Table 1 below.

Table 1: CALL stages (after Pérez Gutiérrez & Pérez Torres, 2005: 562)

	Technology	**Pedagogical Approaches**	**Role of the computer**
Behaviorist CALL (60s-70s)	Mainframe computers	Behaviorism	Tutor
Communicative CALL (80s)	Personal computers	Cognitivism	Tutor and Tool
Integrative CALL (90s-)	Multimedia World Wide Web	Sociocognitivism Constructivism	

The introduction of multimodality and the Internet in this last phase is precisely what has caused CALL as a general label to be called into question and competing terms to arise. Kern & Warschauer (2000: 1), for instance, speak of network-based language teaching (NBLT) to refer to a new side of CALL, "where human communication is the focus". Gassó (2000) alludes to technology-enhanced language learning (TELL) as the latest acronym, coined to signal the incorporation of multimedia and the Internet. And Pennock-Speck (2013) mentions ICT as the preferred paradigm. CALL is associated in all these cases with pre-network language teaching and learning and the use of inflexible programs and mechanical activities with no room for creativity or peer interaction (Pennock-Speck, 2013).

However, these views have been countered by Levy & Hubbard (2005) and Levy & Stockwell (2006). They make a strong case for CALL as the global descriptor for the use of technology in language teaching and learning, built around three main reasons: it distinctively captures the application of technology to language as an object of learning; it reliably describes what we do; and it is an inclusive, established, and stable term which has been longer-lasting and more widespread than any other comparable acronym. Favoring the proliferation of other labels is counterproductive and simply serves to fragment the field, confuse, and distract. Thus, as Levy & Hubbard (2005: 148) maintain, "In the final analysis, the term CALL is simply useful. Avoiding the term simply fuels the idea that CALL is somehow locked into some kind of 1980s, pre-network time warp. The facts prove otherwise".

Despite the controversy aroused by CALL as a general label, what remains incontrovertible is that technology is here to stay (Sharma, 2006: 59) and that its potential to enhance language learning is enormous: "it is obvious that we have entered a new information age in which the links between technology and TEFL have already been established" (Lee, 2000). O'Dell (2004: 6) terms it "the IT revolution" and expounds on how it "has had a particularly significant influence on how TEFL has changed over the last quarter of a century" (2004: 5). CALL has impacted what we teach (computer corpora and concordancing software have brought about striking advances in the grammar and lexis of spoken English); how we teach and how our students learn (by reading and listening to real language and using it productively in email or chat); and how we relate to each other (by availing teachers of opportunities to communicate with other practitioners worldwide).

CALL has also reconfigured teacher and learner roles: the former become facilitators, tutors, and advisors, while the latter need to be more autonomous, active, collaborative, and constructive in their own learning (Gassó, 2000). Thorne & Payne (2005: 380) go as far as to claim that the new generation of IT users "… thinks, performs, learns and communicates in ways that quantitatively differ from cohorts born prior to the wide adoption of digital communication and information technologies". It is what Prensky (2001) refers to as the digital immigrant/digital native divide. Digital natives think and process information in a substantially different way from their predecessors:

> Digital Natives are used to receiving information really fast. They like to parallel process and multi-task. They prefer their graphics *before* their text rather than the opposite. They prefer random access (like hypertext). They function best when networked. They thrive on instant gratification and frequent rewards. They prefer games to "serious" work.

However, both Ware (2009) and O'Dowd (2007) approach these claims with heed for two main reasons: students' acceptance of online activities will depend on whether they see them as relevant, and a gap may exist between their everyday online practices and the online literacies required to function effectively in virtual foreign language learning scenarios. In this sense, there is an increasingly consensual view in the specialized literature (Dudeney, 2011; O'Dowd, 2007; Ware, 2009) that students are not as technology-savvy as Prensky (2001) would have it. The digital immigrant/digital native divide is in fact being superseded by the digital visitor/digital resident dichotomy (Dudeney, 2011), which reflects the increasingly widespread view that students' technological literacy is more limited or patchy than it might seem at first blush: they are tech-comfy (they have the computer literacy to use a digital tools for everyday social and entertainment purposes) but not tech-savvy (which involves being able to use key tools for educational and professional purposes) (Pegrum, 2009).

The impact of CALL has also been intensely felt in the variegated materials and technological options it has spawned for language teaching: "CALL has grown along both the horizontal and vertical axes: It has become a rich and diverse area of work with considerable depth" (Levy & Stockwell, 2006: 1). These options have, in turn, spurred on phenomenal amounts of research into their potential and effectiveness for language learning and teaching: "this volume of activity has led to the production of a sizable corpus of work. In fact, the breadth and diversity of CALL is frequently underestimated" (Levy & Stockwell 2006: xi). Following Lee (2000), Pérez Gutiérrez & Pérez Torres (2005), González-Lloret (2010), Moreno Fuentes (2010), or Palacios Maroto (2010), a classification is provided of the different types of CALL tools which have been identified for language teaching (Table 2).

Table 2: Summary of CALL tools

Multimedia software (programs with a fixed content with multimodal –text, images, audio, video– elements)	*Reference software* (e.g. dictionaries and encyclopedias)
	Drill and practice programs (e.g. multimedia CD-ROMs)
	Games and simulation programs (where students have to make a decision in order to obtain a reward or go on to the next level)
Word processors	Modifying, comprehending, or producing actions can be carried out with them
Software	*User software* (programs ready to be installed and used)
	Programming or authoring software (e.g. Hot Potatoes or JCLIC)
The World Wide Web	Source of *authentic materials and content information* through Internet searches (e.g. Treasure hunts, Webquests, Google Earth)
	Source of *specific language materials* (grammar and vocabulary content pages, online dictionaries, meaningful contextualized language activities)
	Source of *communicative and collaborative tools*: computer-mediated communication

	Synchronous: Chats, voice and videoconferencing, social networks (Facebook, Tuenti, Twitter)	*Asynchronous*: email, forums, electronic lists, newsgroups, web-logs, wikis, pod-casts
	Simulations, virtual worlds, and MMOGS (massively multiplayer online gaming spaces)	

Numerous assets have been associated to the use of these CALL tools for foreign language learning:

- They provide learner-centered environments with increased opportunities for student participation and interaction (Freiermuth, 2002; O'Dowd, 2007; O'Rourke, 2005; Tudini, 2003), thereby helping to establish an important sense of community (Fleming *et al.*, 2002; Rovai, 2002; White, 2006).
- They furnish sufficient and comprehensible input (Doughty & Varela, 1998; Gass, 1998, 2003; VanPatten & Cadierno, 1993;) which is elaborated and not merely simplified (Oh, 2001; Parker & Chaudron, 1987; Yano, Long & Ross, 1994).
- They promote learn by doing (Lee, 2000), engaging students in the negotiation of language based on meaning, and using tasks rather than grammar-based activities (Doughty & Long, 2003; Long, 1985).
- They produce pushed output which allows for the comparison of patterns and the adjustment of interlanguage structures (Swain, 1985, 1995; Swain & Lapkin, 1995).
- They provide immediate feedback (Lalande, 1982; Kubota, 2001).
- They result in increased student autonomy, motivation, and achievement, strengthening linguistic skills, positively affecting learner attitudes, and promoting self-confidence (Lee, 2000; Moreno Fuentes, 2010; Pérez Gutiérrez & Pérez Torres, 2005).

However, the use of technology can also be frought with frustation; as O'Dell (2004: 6) puts it, "Revolution does not come without a cost: two steps forward, one step back". According to this author, Lee (2000), Pérez Gutiérrez & Pérez Torres (2005), and Moreno Fuentes (2010), the following barriers or objections to the use of CALL in the language classrooms must be borne in mind:

- Hardware, software maintenance, and staff development are expensive.
- Computer hardware and software may not always be available.
- Using CALL in the classroom can be potentially time-consuming and may present technological *hiccups*.
- It requires additional knowledge which some teachers might be resilient to acquire. In this sense, the acceptance of technologies by tecnophobe teachers is a particularly tall order.
- Methodological readjustments need to be effected in the curriculum to make learning more autonomous and student-centered.
- Keeping up to speed with the constant and rapid changes involved in the use of CALL necessitates flexibility and adaptability on the part of both the teacher and the students: "engaging in CALL is a continuing challenge that requires time and commitment" (Lee, 2000). In this sense, O'Dell (2004) speaks of the Information Overload Syndrome.

Thus, the success with which CALL is incorporated into the language classroom is eminently reliant on the teacher, which substantiates the view that computers "will not replace teachers, but will supplement their efforts" (Lee, 2000). Technology is no "'silver bullet' which will bring about change and innovation by itself" (O'Dowd, 2007: 33); it is the teacher who needs to set up the program, assign the material, and ultimately hone the course to create an optimal language learning environment through the use of CALL options (Pérez Gutiérrez & Pérez Torres, 2005; Sharma, 2006). In Gassó's (2000: 54) words, "The effectiveness of CALL does not reside in the medium itself but rather on how it is put to use".

In this sense, Pennock-Speck (2013) sets forth three conditions for the use of ICT. The first of them (*Ceffort*) is that it should not be too time-consuming for teachers to design and put into practice activities and methodologies dependent on new technologies, nor should they involve an inordinate workload for the students. Either of these outcomes would inevitably lead to frustration and the rejection of ICT. Secondly, it should not be too expensive (*CEcon*), as this would mean resilience on the part of universities to subsidize its use. In this sense, it is important to invest not only in hardware and software, but especially in what Pegrum (2009: 53) terms "wetware"; that is, the human competence essential to make the most of technology. Thirdly, and perhaps the most important condition, is that ICT should be used only if it brings something new or innovative to teaching practice or gives the students more opportunities to acquire the knowledge and competencies they need (*CInnov*). Contravening any of these conditions, the author claims, will mean the ICT activity will either be superfluous, redundant, or counterproductive –or all of the above. However, if they are met and the use of ICT is adequate, it is highly likely that computer-based language-learning tools will become both pervasive and invisible (Beatty, 2003), leading to what Bax (2003) terms the normalization of CALL, where "technology is invisible [...] hardly even recognized as technology".

This is precisely what the present monograph seeks to contribute to: fostering the successful incorporation of digital competence in Bologna-adapted language degrees. To this end, it pools the insights of a set of international practitioners and investigators who report on classroom- and research-based experiences which have integrated ICT for specific and generic competence development within the Higher Education (HE) language context. It begins by framing the topic against the broader backdrop of the competencies which the foreign language teacher must acquire and develop with the new European HE arena. This is analyzed by **Daniel Madrid-Fernández**, who probes different competency-based approaches within the European context. The basic competencies within the Spanish education system are brought to the fore, along with the pedagogical implications of recent legislative developments. In addition to this, the chapter offers an array of cross-curricular competencies to be developed by teachers in general, and language teaching professionals in particular, as well as a series of guidelines for a competency-based assessment of language curricula.

A specific teacher training experience in the use of Web 2.0 tools is then reported on by **Anna Franca Plastina**. Her chapter describes an experimental study carried out at the University of Calabria (Italy) with the aim of preparing future EFL teachers for the lifelong process of competency development in e-Europe. Both quantitative and qualitative findings in the pre- and post-training phases of the experiment underpin the hypothesis that it is possible to narrow the current European ICT-skills gap in local educational settings by offering transformational guidance enabling teachers to adopt a European approach to their praxis.

Web 2.0 tools –concretely, the educational social network site NING– are also explored in **Anna María Brígido-Corachán & María Goretti Zaragoza-Ninet**'s chapter. In their case study, they analyze the impact of this site on an upper-level ESL module at the University of Valencia (Spain), offering detailed information about the didactic advantages provided by this multimodal online tool, which integrates digital literacies with the creative practice of writing, reading and listening activities in the English language. Their results show that the use of this educational platform greatly improved their students' digital, communicative, and collaborative skills.

If these authors' research has evinced that digital competence can act as a catalyst for the development of other linguistic and generic competencies of crucial relevance in HE language degrees, so do the next set of contributions. The use of ICT to develop the multiple literacies involved in digital competence, linguistic skills, cooperative learning, critical thinking, or literary aspects is explored in the contributions by Maruenda-Bataller & Clavel-Arroitia; Talaván, Bárcena, & Villarroel; Rodríguez-Arancón & Jordano-de la Torre; and Borham-Puyal & Olmos-Migueláñez. In their chapter, **Sergio Maruenda-Bataller & Begoña Clavel-Arroitia** describe their experience in the use of blended-learning methodology at the University of Valencia (Spain), and they point out the advantages and drawbacks of the implementation of ICT in the English class. They provide data concluding that its implementation has acted as a powerful catalyst for higher achievement. Likewise, **Noa Talaván, Elena Bárcena, & Álvaro Villarroel** highlight the benefits of competence transfer between different groups of English students (Tourism and English Philology) undertaking computer supported collaborative language learning (namely, doubling and subtitling a tourism video) at the National Distance Education University (Spain). **Pilar Rodríguez-Arancón & María Jordano-de la Torre** report on a pedagogical innovation experience at the same university which addresses the need to undertake appropriate development of comprehension and production skills in English by making students work, through telecollaboration, with English-speaking individuals from other countries. Literary Studies is, on the other hand, the main focus of analysis in the chapter by **Miriam Borham-Puyal & Susana Olmos-Migueláñez**, who describe the design of original resources and instruments built into the virtual platform Moodle, aimed at the development and assessment of reading efficiency and competence in critical analysis.

Finally, assessment of such competencies comes to the fore in the aforementioned chapters by Madrid-Fernández and Maruenda-Bataller & Clavel-Arroitia, but it is more specifically targeted in that by **Kent Löfgren**, which addresses university teachers' evaluations of their students' competencies. He also delves into the historical roots behind student-centered education and competency development fostered in the EHEA, thus offering the necessary contextualization so as to make personal choices in the shift from older methodologies to the new winds of change coming from Bologna.

Thus, the contributions included in the present volume seem to make a compelling case for the incorporation of ICT into the new language learning scenario provided by the implementation of the European Credit Transfer System. In the light of these findings, the use of technology should not be seen, as Kessler & Ware (2013: 104) put it, "as a separate competency, but rather as a vehicle for accomplishing other tasks". Whether we like it or not, ICT is here to stay, and its role is becoming increasingly significant in our HE system: "If our university and state universities in general are to remain at the forefront in teaching and research in the future, we have to make sure that we implement ICT as effectively as possible in the new degree and postgraduate degree structures" (Pennock-Speck, 2009: 183-184). The experiences and studies comprised in this volume will hopefully help us make strides in this direction and open a window into the many possibilities which ICT has to offer in Higher Education.

Bibliography

Bailey, P. D. (2008). Should "teacher centred teaching" replace "student centred learning". *Chemistry, Education and Research Practices 9*, 70-74.

Bax, S. (2003). CALL - past, present and future. *System 31*, 13-28.

Beatty, K. (2003). *Teaching and Researching Computer-Assisted Language Learning.* Harlow: Pearson Education Limited.

Benito, A., & Cruz, A. (2007). *Nuevas claves para la docencia universitaria en el Espacio Europeo de Educación Superior*. Madrid: Narcea.

Doughty, C., & Long, M. H. (2003). Optimal psycholinguistic environments for distance foreign language learning. *Language Learning & Technology 7*(3), 50-80.

Doughty, C., & Varela, E. (1998). Communicative focus-on-form. In C. Doughty, & J. Williams (Eds.), *Focus-on-Form in Classroom Second Language Acquisition* (pp. 114-138). Cambridge: Cambridge University Press.

Dudeney, G. (2011). New literacies, teachers, and learners. Paper presented at the *34th TESOL-Spain Convention. Changes and Challenges: Expanding Horizons in ELT*, Madrid.

Fleming, S., Hiple, D., & Du, Y. (2002). Foreign language distance education at the University of Hawai'i. In C. A. Spreen (Ed.), *New Technologies and Language Learning: Issues and Options (Technical Report #25)* (pp. 13-54). Honolulu, HI: University of Hawai'i Second Language Teaching & Curriculum Center.

Freiermuth, M. R. (2002). Online chatting: An alternative approach to simulations. *Simulation & Gaming*, *32*(2), 187-195.

Gass, S. (1998). Apples and oranges. Or, why apples are not oranges and don't need to be: A response to Firth and Wagner. *Modern Language Journal*, *82*, 83-90.

Gass, S. (2003). Input and interaction. In C. Doughty, & M. H. Long (Eds.), *Handbook of Second Language Acquisition* (pp. 224-255). New York: Basil Blackwell.

Gassó, E. (2000). *Computer Assisted Language Learning*. New York: Fundación Universitaria Iberoamericana.

González-Lloret, M. (2010). Technology for language teaching: The future has started. Invited talk at the University of Jaén. January 18th, 2010.

Kern, R., & Warschauer, M. (2000). Introduction: Theory and practice of network-based language teaching. In M. Warschauer, & R. Kern (Eds.), *Network-based Language Teaching: Concepts and Practice* (pp. 1-19). Cambridge: Cambridge University Press.

Kessler, G., & Ware, P. D. (2013). Addressing the language classroom competencies of the European Higher Education Area through the use of technology. In M. L. Pérez Cañado (Ed.), *Competency-based Language Teaching in Higher Education* (pp. 93-105). Amsterdam: Springer.

Kubota, M. (2001). Error correction strategies used by learners of Japanese when revising a writing task. *System 29*(4), 467-80.
Lalande, J. F. (1982). Reducing composition errors: An experiment. *Modern Language Journal 66*, 140-149.
Lee, K. (2000). English teachers' barriers to the use of computer-assisted language learning. *The Internet TESL Journal VI*(12). Retrieved from http://iteslj.org/Articles/Lee-CALLbarriers.html (01/01/2013).
Levy, M. (1997). *Computer-Assisted Language Learning. Context and Conceptualization.* Oxford: Oxford University Press.
Levy, M., & Hubbard, H. (2005). Why call CALL "CALL"? *Computer Assisted Language Learning, 18*(3), 143-149.
Levy, M., & Stockwell, G. (2006). *CALL Dimensions. Options and Issues in Computer-Assisted Language Learning.* New Jersey: Lawrence Erlbaum Associates.
Long, M. H. (1985). A role for instruction in second language acquisition: Task-based language teaching. In K. Hyltenstam, & M. Pienemann (Eds.), *Modeling and Assessing Second Language Acquisition* (pp. 77-99). Clevedon: Multilingual Matters.
Moreno Fuentes, E. (2010). FUNtastic writing: Using wikis and blogs in the language classroom. In M. L. Pérez Cañado (Ed.), *Proceedings of the XXIII GRETA Convention. Updating TEFL: A Classic Reborn* (pp. 33-46). Jaén: Joxman.
Oh, S. Y. (2001). Two types of input modification and EFL reading comprehension: Simplification versus elaboration. *TESOL Quarterly, 35*(1), 69-96.
O'Dell, F. (2004). The IT revolution. *English Teaching Professional, 32*, 4-6.
O'Dowd, R. (2007). Foreign language education and the rise of on-line communication: A review of promises and realties. In R. O'Dowd (Ed.), *Online Intercultural Exchange* (pp. 17-40). Exeter: Multilingual Matters.
O'Rourke, B. (2005). Form-focused interaction in online tandem learning. *CALICO Journal, 22*(3), 433-466.
Palacios Maroto, L. M. (2010). This text is hyperb! (or how to use online applications to practise writing). In M. L. Pérez Cañado (Ed.), *Proceedings of the XXIII GRETA Convention. Updating TEFL: A Classic Reborn* (pp. 47-52). Jaén: Joxman.
Parker, K., & Chaudron, C. (1987). The effects of linguistic simplification and elaborative modifications on L2 comprehension. *University of Hawai'i Working Papers in ESL, 6*, 107-133.
Pegrum, M. (2009). *From Blogs to Bombs. The Future of Digital Technologies in Education.* Crawley: UWA Publishing.
Pennock-Speck, B. (2008). The implementation of ICT in the second-cycle History of the English Language module at the Universitat de València. *GRETA. Revista para Profesores de Inglés, 16*, 65-70.
Pennock-Speck, B. (2009). European convergence and the role of ICT in English Studies at the Universitat de València: Lessons learned and prospects for the future. In M. L. Pérez Cañado (Ed.), *English Language Teaching in the European Credit Transfer System: Facing the Challenge* (pp. 169-185). Frankfurt am Main: Peter Lang.
Pennock-Speck, B. (2013). Teaching competences through ICTs in an English degree programme in a Spanish setting. In M. L. Pérez Cañado (Ed.), *Competency-based Language Teaching in Higher Education* (pp. 107-118). Amsterdam: Springer.

Pérez Cañado, M. L. (2010). English Language Teaching in the European Higher Education Area: From policy to practice. *International Journal of Innovation in Language Learning and Teaching 4*(1), 53-69.

Pérez Gutiérrez, M., & Pérez Torres, I. 2005. Audio-visual resources and new technologies in ELT. In N. McLaren, D. Madrid, & A. Bueno (Eds.), *TEFL in Secondary Education* (pp. 546-578). Granada: Universidad de Granada.

Prensky, M. (2001). Digital natives, digital immigrants. *On the Horizon, 9*(5). Retrieved from http://www.marcprensky.com/writing/Prensky%20-%20Digital%20Natives,%20Digital%20Immigrants%20-%20Part1.pdf. (01/01/2013).

Rovai, A. P. (2002). Development of an instrument to measure classroom community. *The Internet and Higher Education, 5*, 197-211.

Sharma, P. (2006). Future in the balance. *English Teaching Professional, 42*, 58-59.

Swain, M. (1985). Communicative competence: Some roles of comprehensible input and comprehensible output in its development. In S. Gass, & C. Madden (Eds.), *Input in Second Language Acquisition* (pp. 235-256). New York: Newbury House.

Swain, M. (1995). Three functions of output in second language learning. In G. Cook, & B. Seidlhofer (Eds.), *Principle and Practice in Applied Linguistics* (pp. 125-144). Oxford: Oxford University Press.

Swain, M., & Lapkin, S. (1995). Problems in output and the cognitive processes they generate: A step towards second language learning. *Applied Linguistics, 16*, 371-391.

Thorne, S. L., & Payne, J. S. (2005). Evolutionary trajectories, internet-mediated expression, and language education. *The CALICO Journal, 22*, 371-397.

Tudini, V. (2003). Using native speakers in chat. *Language Learning & Technology* 7(3), 141-159.

VanPatten, B., & Cadierno, T. (1993). Input processing and second language acquisition: A role for instruction. *The Modern Language Journal, 77*, 45-57.

Ware, P. D. (2009). Critical issues in telecollaborative task design. Invited talk within the University of Jaén ECTS Seminar Program. February 10th, 2009.

Warschauer, M., & Healey, D. (1998). Computers and language learning: An overview. *Language Teaching, 31*, 57-71.

White, C. (2006). State of the art: Distance learning of foreign languages. *Language Teaching, 39*(4), 247-264.

Yano, Y., Long, M. H., & Ross, S. (1994). The effects of simplified and elaborated texts on foreign language reading comprehension. *Language Learning, 44*(2): 189-219.

The New Competency-based Foreign Language Teacher Education in the European Context

Daniel Madrid-Fernández

Abstract

In this chapter a special emphasis is placed on competence-based approaches within the European context. In the ensuing sections, I define the key conceptual aspects which accompany this type of approach and focus more closely on the basic competences proposed within the Spanish education system. I also examine the characteristics of these competences, along with the pedagogical implications of recent legislative developments.

In addition to this, I present a series of cross-curricular competences to be developed by teachers (including instrumental, personal and systemic competences). I also examine those competences which are common to all teacher profiles (*savoir*, *savoir faire* and *savoir être*), as well as a series of competences specific to language teaching professionals (including classroom management, professional competences and transnational competences). This is followed by a series of possible guidelines for the evaluation of a curriculum based on competences which considers several factors to be taken into account and types of instruments to be used in assessment. Finally, a critical appreciation of this type of approach is provided and possible areas of improvement based on the works of other authors are examined.

Competency-based teacher education

The competency-based movement enjoys a long tradition. Originally, it was influenced by behaviourist theory, which came to prominence in the seventies. This approach became popular in the USA when it was used for teacher training under the name *competency-based teacher education* (CBTE). In the nineties, it continued to be used in the British national vocational education qualification system and other similar movements which were concerned with the definition of adequate standards of competence and professional profiles for a global world economy. From 2000 to 2003, the Organisation for Cooperation and Economic Development (OECD) developed its DeSeCo project (Definition and Selection of Competencies), and used the concept of competence in a more comprehensive way and with different connotations (Rychen & Salganik, 2001, 2003). It provided a new conceptual framework and identified some key competencies which helped to define the desirable goals of education systems and lifelong learning. After that, the European Union, and Spain in particular, reformulated the school curriculum around the powerful though polemic and complex concept of competence.

Although some authors have drawn a distinction between *competency* and *competence*, in this paper the two terms are used interchangeably. *Competency* (actual performance) refers more precisely to skills employees must have or acquire to achieve high levels of performance. It thus focuses on the person. Based on someone's competencies, we can distinguish superior performers from average or poor performers. In turn, the term *competence* (potential to perform) focuses on the job and refers to a set of minimum standards; that is, the basic requirement to perform a job. A person's competence is demonstrated by occupational standards, performance and outputs. It is the potential to perform something or a demonstrated skill in performing an actual task.

Since the DeSeCo project, several countries have developed competence-based curricula with a variety of designations: basic capacities and technological capacities (France), basic skills (USA), core skills, industry specific standards (Great Britain), key competences (Australia), etc. Adopted as *basic competencies* in Spain, the concept of *key competencies* as the fundamental curricular axis is consolidated following the definitions in the OECD document (Rychen & Salganik, 2003). This document defines competence as the capacity to respond to complex demands and carry out a variety of tasks in an adequate manner. It entails a combination of practical skills, knowledge, motivation, ethical values, attitudes, emotions, social and behavioural operations that are activated in order to attain successful outcomes to an enterprise (see Pérez Gómez, 2007: 10).

The behavioural CBTE approach

For CBTE, teacher training based on competencies is more reductionist, atomised and lineal. Three basic criteria are used to assess the trainee's teaching behaviour and effectiveness: i.e., knowledge, performance and outcome. (Arends, Masla, & Weber, 1971). According to most authors (see http://www.reproline.jhu.edu/english/6read/6training/cbt/cbt.htm#Characteristics), the main characteristics of CBTE are:

- a careful choice of training competencies,
- the integration of theory with the practice and performance of skills; learning should be self-paced,
- the use of a variety of support materials including print, audiovisual and simulations (models) to develop the planned skills and competences,
- an outline of the knowledge and skills to be achieved,
- the satisfactory completion of training based on the achievement of specified competencies by trainees,
- flexible grouping techniques including large group methods, small group activities and individual study are essential,
- completion of training is based on achievement of all specified competencies.

The behavioural interpretation of training considers competencies as operational and observable actions that have little connection with underlying mental processes. Furthermore, behaviourism gives little importance to the interactive and complex nature of tasks. It ignores the mental operations that underlie behaviour, intentions, and actions, and does not take into account the significance of contextual factors, and the effects of their ethical and interpersonal aspects. Behavioural objectives are set up, developed in the classroom and assessed from a perspective external to the individual concerned. In this process, teachers simply check to what extent operational and instructional objectives have been achieved by learners (Madrid, 1996).

However, becoming competent requires much more than this. It depends on people's capacities to recognise, analyse and solve innovative and complex daily life situations. In order to do that, we need to activate all the abilities, skills, knowledge, strategies, attitudes and values at our disposal.

The new competency-based teacher education movement

At present, competencies must be developed and evaluated from an internal perspective; that is, from the subjects' points of view. Their description emphasises subjective aspects, trying to understand the subjects' internal attitudes, behaviour, values and motivations. In this sense, competencies are conceived as a set of socio-affective, sensory, psychomotor aspects and cognitive abilities that allow people to carry out adequately a role, function, activity or task. Being competent depends on people's potential to recognise, analyse and solve current daily life situations, as well as more innovative and complex ones. In order to do that, all the abilities, skills, knowledge, strategies, attitudes and values at our disposal must be activated.

Based on socio-cultural and constructivist studies of human development and learning capacity, the competence approach starts from the premise that subjects make judgements, revise them, reflect on and change their behaviour when they reconstruct their relevant knowledge and interact with other people in the complex contexts of social relations. Recent studies have argued that individual abilities are social constructions and reflect the cultural practices that accompany the contexts and situations surrounding human activities.

Authors that have dealt with this topic (Gimeno Sacristán *et al.*, 2008; Pérez Gómez, 2007; Pérez González, 2009; Rial Sánchez, 2007; Rychen & Salganik, 2001, 2003; amongst others), agree that *competencies* are formed by the integration of *knowledge* (directed to information processing and application), *skills and abilities* (know-how), and *strategies* (ways of achieving things and solving problems). In addition, they include *attitudes and values*, which generate the moods people experience when dealing with personal conflicts arising from their current situations, and which explain the importance given to daily life events. Hipkins (2006) and Blanco Blanco (2007) have also argued that competences integrate knowledge, skills or abilities, attitudes and values.

Consequently, the present concept of *competence* includes cognitive and non-cognitive dimensions: knowledge, cognitive abilities, practical skills, attitudes, values and emotions. Hence, this new concept goes beyond the behaviourist orientation, taking into consideration the complexity of the inner structure of a person's actions, the set of mental attributes that maintain people's voluntary actions and capacities in different contexts and situations.

Gimeno Sacristán (2008: 36) has illustrated the conceptual scope of competence and the ways in which it overlaps with other related concepts in the following graph:

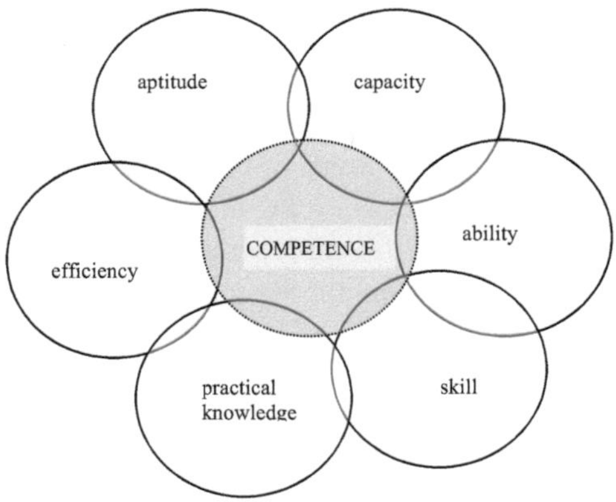

Fig. 1: Intersection of competence with other related concepts

Tobón (2005) and Rial Sánchez (2007) have proposed several structural components in the formulation or enunciation of a competence:

- A description of the competence.
- *Performance criteria*: i.e., expected results in real life situations.
- *Application level*: i.e., execution criteria.
- *Problems* to be solved.
- *Specific elements* implied in each competence.
- *Basic knowledge* required to attain results.

- *Skills* required to evaluate the competence.
- *Some possible strategies* associated with its performance.

When setting up competences, Goñi Zabala (2007: 117) proposes the integration of three basic components: a) a mental operation plus b) object (knowledge) plus c) the aim to be accomplished. An example of competence that integrates these three elements might be: a) the ability to select (mental operation); b) learning materials (object); c) that allow the completion of authentic tasks in class (objective/aim) (see also Angulo, 2008: 193).

Basic competencies

The concept of *competence* or being *competent* refers to someone's ability to cope effectively in a specific professional domain. It subsumes the concepts of aptitude, capacity and disposition. The Spanish Organic Law 5/2002, June 19, on professional qualifications and vocational training defines *competence* (art. 7.3.b) as the integration of knowledge and capacities whose goal is the realization of professional objectives.

Furthermore, the theory related to learning through competencies (Competency Based Training) gives professional preparation a multi-dimensional character, by integrating three types of knowledge: *theoretical knowledge* (principles and facts), *practical knowledge* (abilities and skills), *existential competence* (*savoir-faire*, attitudes and values) (see CEF, 2001: 104-105). This concept of basic competences is inherent in the definition of the European Union's *key competencies*.

The DeSeCo project has selected three large spheres from which key competencies are derived. These three areas, in turn, are related to the generic learning domains established by Delors' report (UNESCO, 1996), the three curricular axes proposed by the LOGSE (1990) and the general competences established by the CEF (2001), as illustrated in Table 1 below:

Table 1: Large spheres of key competences

LOGSE, 1990	***UNESCO, 1996***	***DeSeCo Project, 2000/2003***	***CEF, 2001***
Concepts	Learning to know	Use of interactive tools	Declarative knowledge
Procedures	Learning to do		Skills and know-how

Attitudes	Learning to live together	Interaction with other groups	Existential competence
	Learning to be	Autonomous work	Ability to learn

In the OECD document and European guidelines for future educational policies, *key competencies* comprise knowledge, abilities, skills and attitudes. These are transferable and multi-functional; each person needs them for his/her development, integration and employment; and they should have been developed by the end of the school period in order to constitute a basis for life-long learning (see Jiménez Benítez, 2006).

The concept of *basic competences* coincides with the *key competencies* defined by the European Union Working Group in 2002. As they are defined in Royal Decree (R.D. 1513/2006), 7 December, (BOE nº293 de 08-12-2006), the eight basic competences comprise:

a) linguistic communication competence (including L1 and additional languages)
b) mathematical competence
c) knowledge and interaction with the physical and natural world
d) treatment of digital information
e) social and civic competence
f) cultural and artistic competence
g) learning to learn throughout life
h) personal autonomy and initiative.

Other education systems, such as those in Australia, Canada and the USA, have also proposed eight basic competencies, in which the following abilities may be integrated (Argudín, 2007): 1) Estimation, 2) Communication, 3) Critical thinking, 4) Social relations, 5) Functionality, 6) Leadership, 7) Research and Teaching, 8) Knowledge integration.

The previously mentioned competencies run closely parallel to the *multiple intelligences* established by Gardner (1983, 1999, 2001). For him, human cognitive ability comprises at least eight different frames or intelligences some of which are very similar to the key competences indicated in Table 2 below:

Table 2: Gardner's intelligences and the basic/key competences

Gardner's Intelligences	***Definitions***	***Key competences***
A. Musical-rhythmic	Ability to perceive and appreciate rhythm, pitch and melody	Cultural and artistic competence
B. Verbal-linguistic	The ability to use oral and written language effectively and creatively	Competence in linguistic communication
C. Visual-spatial	The ability to represent the spatial world internally	(not mentioned)
D. Naturalist	The ability to discriminate among living things, as well as to have sensitivity towards the natural world	Knowledge and interaction with the physical and natural world
E. Bodily-kinaesthetic	Ability to use the body to express oneself, to handle physical objects with dexterity	(not mentioned)
F. Interpersonal	The ability to understand other people, to work co-operatively and to communicate verbally and non-verbally with others	Social and civic competence
G. Intrapersonal	The ability to understand the internal aspects of the self and to practise self-discipline	Autonomy and personal initiative
H. Logical-mathematical	The ability to use numbers effectively, to recognise abstract patterns, to discern relationships and to reason well	Mathematical reasoning

Two basic competences, digital competence and learning throughout life in an autonomous way, do not appear in Gardner's multiple intelligences scheme.

Main characteristics of basic competencies

Taking into consideration the OECD's DeSeCo Project and its later critical development, some authors have recognised a set of characteristics that *key competencies* share (see Jiménez Benítez, 2006 and Pérez Gómez, 2007: 13):

- *Holistic and integrative orientation.* The combination of knowledge, capacities, skills, attitudes, aptitudes, values and emotions.
- *Dynamic character.* Action and performance operations implied.
- *Learner-centredness.* Students are considered the main agents of their own learning, and are able to organise and monitor it.
- *Multifunctional character.* A variety of objectives can be achieved.
- *Process orientation.* They are more process- than product-oriented.
- *Contextual focus.* They are linked to different contexts of action.
- *Ethical dimension.* Their development implies a set of values and attitudes during their developmental process throughout life.
- *Creative character of transference.* Transference is conceived as a creative process in each context.
- *Reflective character.* A permanent reflective process is required in order to harmonise learners' intentions with the possibilities of each context.
- *Evolutionary nature.* They change through life's stages and may be developed, improved, spoiled or restricted.

In sum, it can be said that being *competent* implies knowing how to do things in a complex, adaptable and reflective way, in a variety of contexts. It involves the integration of knowledge, procedures, attitudes and values whose mastery and application change throughout life. Key or basic competences are valid for the whole population, regardless of their sex, social, cultural and family condition.

Among the pedagogical and curricular implications of the competence-based approach, Pérez Gómez has highlighted the following (2007: 23):

- The main concern of education is not transmitting knowledge, but *developing competences*, abilities and skills. This idea started to be emphasised with the LOGSE in 1990, as well as the organization of the school curriculum around concepts, procedures and attitudes.
- The students' *construction* of their mental models and schemata are important objectives of teaching.

- For key competences to favour significant knowledge the active involvement of students in searching, studying, experimentation, reflection and application is necessary.
- The development of basic competences implies the continuous implementation of real and *authentic tasks* and their connection with daily life and social environment.
- Teaching and learning in our present changing world demand the development of techniques and strategies for *learning how to learn*.
- Significant learning involves the development of the students' *meta-cognition* and their capacity to control and regulate their own learning processes.
- *Cooperative learning* is a desirable and powerful learning technique.
- Evaluation must have a *formative* orientation.
- Teachers must act as mediators and *facilitators of learning* incorporating systematic tutorial sessions and providing positive feedback to the students.

General competencies for teachers

A broad range of competencies is considered useful for all occupations. This implies the integration of several aptitudes, personality traits, knowledge and acquired values. In the university context, they may have the following benefits:

- Increasing the connection between academic institutions and the job market.
- Establishing a closer relation between what academic life offers and professional work demands.
- Providing an integrated preparation of professionals.

The Spanish Agency for Quality in Education (ANECA) has established the following competencies for teacher education (2005):

a) *Instrumental competencies* (they act as a tool to attain specific aims)

- Ability to analyse and synthesise
- Capacity to organise and plan
- Oral and written communication in the mother tongue
- Knowledge of relevant ICT to the area of study
- Ability to manage information
- Problem-solving skills
- Decision-making skills

b) *Personal competencies* (they help people establish social interaction with others)

- Teamwork
- Interdisciplinary teamwork

- Working in an international context
- Interpersonal skills
- Recognition of diversity and multiculturalism
- Critical reasoning
- Ethical commitment

c) *Systemic competencies* (these are competencies related to the understanding of the whole system; they require a combination of imagination, sensitivity and an ability to relate parts to the whole)

- Autonomous learning
- Adaptation to new situations
- Creativity
- Leadership
- Knowledge of other cultures and customs
- Initiative and entrepreneurship
- Motivation for quality
- Sensitivity towards environmental issues

Specific competencies for foreign language teachers

Foreign Language (FL) teachers need to develop specific skills such as selecting adequate content and learning activities, presenting, exploiting and evaluating them in class, activating interaction between the students, establishing an overall balance between constituents, dealing with errors, promoting autonomous work, paying attention to diversity, etc.

The competences that FL teachers develop in their initial and in-service preparation stages must allow them to operate within the paradigmatic framework that has emerged in the last decades (Jacobs & Farrell, 2001). These competencies include:

- Ensuring a learner-centred FL curriculum.
- Paying attention to both learning processes and final products.
- Paying attention to diversity and the social nature of learning.
- Contextualising teaching and learning situations.
- Promoting holistic learning.
- Developing the students' meta-cognition.
- Encouraging autonomous work.
- Favouring significant learning.
- Promoting life-long learning strategies.
- Encouraging learning through discovery.

- Encouraging cooperative learning.
- Seeking opportunities for professional development.

Within the competency-based teacher education paradigm, the ANECA has provided a list of specific professional competencies to help FL teachers achieve the objectives established by the Central and Autonomous Administration (see Bueno, McLaren, & Madrid, 2005: 29-30; Madrid & Hughes, 2009: 229-230; Madrid & McLaren, 2004: 24-26; Vez, 2007: 36-37) based on a group of 868 informants who graded the importance of each competence for teaching and learning foreign languages at school. The scale ranged from 1 (low) to 4 (high) and the mean score is given in brackets (see ANECA, 2005: 83; Madrid & Hughes, 2011):

Competencies related to disciplinary knowledge (knowing)

1. To have mastery in *communicative competence* as well as good linguistic knowledge and socio-cultural knowledge of the target language (3.7).
2. To know the main pedagogical trends and *methods* in foreign language teaching for children, as well as their application in the FL classroom at the different levels established in the curriculum (3.2).
3. To know the cognitive and linguistic bases for the *acquisition* of first and additional languages (3.0).
4. To have sufficient communicative competence in at least one *other EU language* (English, French, German, Italian, etc.) or language from other countries (Arabic, Russian, Chinese, etc.) (2.1).

Professional competences (knowing how)

5. To be able to *plan* what is to be taught and assessed, as well as to create and develop teaching strategies, types of activities and class materials (3.5).
6. To design *activities* intended to promote sufficient *oral and written communication* by students in the new language, establishing individual plans for those students who need them (3.49).
7. To develop general, linguistic and communicative competencies progressively in students, through the integrated practice of *concepts*, *procedures* and *attitudes* in the FL class (3.4).
8. To apply diverse ways of *assessing* student learning: planning objectives to be assessed, the degree of success, assessment criteria and instruments, and the points at which assessment will take place (3.1).
9. To assess previous knowledge and needs, introducing different strategies for students at their own levels (*individual differences*) and for the characteristics of the educational context (3.1).

10. To encourage the development of oral and written language, paying special attention to new *technological resources* and elements from distance education (3.1).
11. To be able to encourage the development of metalinguistic/*metacognitive* skills for the acquisition of the new language, through relevant tasks which are meaningful and appropriate for students (3.0).
12. To be able to develop attitudes and positive, open representations towards linguistic and *cultural diversity* in the classroom (3.0).
13. To be receptive towards pupils' *errors* in production/understanding, guiding work through analysis (3.0).
14. To select and design educational *materials* and resources from children's literature in the target language and from written and audiovisual media sources (2.7).
15. To use gestures, expression and *dramatisation* as resources (2.7).

Trans-national competencies

16. To have sufficient knowledge of the *culture(s)* and language being taught, along with its principal manifestations (3.0).
17. To collaborate in, to design and, where appropriate, to guide activities involving *cultural exchange* with residents from other countries, showing management skills in these processes, including local, regional, national and international student and teacher exchange programmes (2.6).

The most important competencies for the informants used by the ANECA's survey are 1) the mastery in *communicative and linguistic competence,* 5) being able to plan *teaching units,* select teaching strategies and activities and prepare class materials and 6) to design *activities* for *oral and written communication.* Thus, the knowledge of the FL and the capacity to teach in a variety of situations seem to be the most important professional competences for future language teachers. Nevertheless, it is surprising that the knowledge of a second foreign language (mean=2.1) and cultural exchanges with residents of other countries (mean=2.6) are ranked in such a low position.

Assessment of competencies

The competency-based paradigm entails important curricular changes which involve new teaching, learning and evaluation techniques in order to discover to what extent trainees have achieved the planned competencies. A variety of evaluation tasks and activities are therefore necessary so that learners can apply the knowledge, procedures and attitudes they have developed in order to demonstrate the competences they have acquired. The link between simply knowing something and being able to put it into practice with positive attitudes is essential.

Though both dimensions are important, from a constructivist point of view, the evaluation of competencies is centred more intensively upon the learning process than upon final results. Therefore, a formative evaluation of tasks through weekly tutorial sessions is essential. With this approach, evaluation results not only include the assignment of grades, but also profiling the students' progress with qualitative statements that describe their levels of proficiency (see Keteke & Roesgiers, 1995).

There are, on the other hand, factors that must be taken into account when establishing the evaluation criteria (see Argudín, 2007). These are:

- The *importance* of competence, related to students' interests, needs and motivation and also to the degree in which the competence contributes to the pre-planned professional profile.
- Its *difficulty*, which to a certain degree represents the effort the students must make to demonstrate the competence attainment indicators.
- Its *scope* and extension, given that competencies involve different concepts, procedures and attitudes the students must acquire to achieve the desired proficiency level.
- The *context* in which the pedagogic activity takes place, which is determined by the group's socio-economic and cultural characteristics and its environmental circumstances.

Evaluation should not be used to censure students' achievement, but to help them understand how they learn and what their difficulties are in order to improve the strategies employed in class. Evaluation should not only address outcomes, but also the fundamental variables that intervene in the teaching and learning process: the *activities* proposed by the teacher, the *content* that the students study and the *learning experiences* in which they participate.

The evaluation process will include a variety of techniques that shows the students' degree of mastery when applying what they have studied in each discipline to real-life situations. The main objective will be to find out their levels of proficiency in each of the professional competencies established for the course.

Among the evaluation techniques that can be applied, the following should be emphasised:

- Classroom observation: participation, interest, commitment to tasks,
- Self-evaluation questionnaires on the course competencies,
- Surveys and quizzes on specific aspects,

- Interviews and oral exams in the L2,
- Written exams/tests,
- Group discussions and debates on certain topics,
- Group work,
- Students' performance in extracurricular activities,
- Classroom diaries,
- Notebooks and written exercises, completion of practical activities,
- Students' papers and essays,
- Students' portfolios,
- Video and audio recordings.

Critique of the competency-based teacher education approach

The competency-based curriculum has been criticised from various viewpoints, especially by authors identified with the progressive movement in education (see Bennett, 1979; Consejo Educativo de Castilla y León, 2007a, 2007b; Gimeno Sacristán, 2008; Vez, 2007). Some of the weak points found in this approach were the following:

- *Unclear definition of terms*. The concepts used are not defined in a clear way. It is very difficult to distinguish the difference between *competence* (or competency) and *capacity*, *ability*, *skill*, *aptitude* and *objective*. A comprehensive approach is adopted and an amalgam of elements is often included in the concept of competence. This is especially complex in operational terms, when trying to apply it to an educational scenario.
- *A lack of coherence between theory and its practical application to professional spheres*. The holistic and integrative character of concepts, procedures and attitudes in competences is not reflected in their use, which is often reduced to one or two words, such as: Creativity, Leadership, Autonomous learning, Interpersonal skills, etc.
- *Education is sometimes conceived as a market (business model of education)*. Some authors have complained that an educational model cannot be based on competencies which have been derived from social, economic, employment and business demands (Angulo, 2008; Gimeno Sacristán, 2008; Torres Santomé, 2008; Vez, 2007). Others have gone further and warned about the risk of converting education into a commercial model whose function is to transmit and reproduce the values of dominant socio-economic groups. Finally, there are yet others who see this approach as neo-positivist and neo-liberal, excessively technical, behaviourist and uncritical in the teacher education sphere (see Consejo Educativo de Castilla y León, 2007a).

- *Reductionist approach.* For some authors, dividing teacher education into a set of competencies is considered too reductionist, partial and unilateral. This critical line is followed by Moreno Moreno & Soto Martínez (2005), who argue in favour of a more diverse approach, such as the multiple intelligences theory proposed by Gardner (1983, 1999, 2011).
- *Behavioural orientation.* Some authors have seen, in the competency-based teacher education model, too much influence of conduct and behaviour *versus* the capacities related to thinking and social transformation (Chappell, 1996). However, if the counter-arguments put forward by Pérez Gómez (2007) are considered, the behaviourist approach of the seventies has been superseded by the new social-constructivist and interactive orientation of present-day competencies.
- *Global and cross-curricular work is not strengthened.* In addition, the definition of competencies is too general and does not refer to specific aspects of students' lives, so that multiple interpretations are possible.
- *There is no sequential and coordinated treatment in the inclusion and follow-up of competencies.* There seems to be a significant lack of coherence between the disciplinary approach of Spanish study plans and their competence-based focus that demands a more cross-curricular orientation. There is a move from disciplines to competencies and not from professional competencies to disciplines, which would be more logical.
- *There is an individualist slant and bias in the approach.* More cooperative, social and interpersonal strategies are ignored. More personal references to emotions and individual development are needed.
- *Evaluation criteria are not clear-cut.* Many competences need to be more clearly expressed, and the expected behaviour needs to be more operational and observable so that it can be evaluated. In this sense, learners would know exactly what is to be assessed. As we can see in the official documents (e.g. ANECA, 2005), this is not the case.

Bibliography

ANECA (2005). *Libro blanco. Título de Grado en Magisterio, vol. I and II.* Madrid: Agencia Nacional de Evaluación de la Calidad y Acreditación.

Angulo, J. F. (2008). La voluntad de distracción: Las competencias en la universidad. In J. Gimeno Sacristán *et al.* (Eds.), *Educar por competencias: ¿Qué hay de nuevo?* (pp. 176-205). Madrid: Morata.

Arends, R. L., Masla, J. A., & Weber, W. A. (1971). *Handbook for the Development of Instructional Modules in Competency-based Teacher Education Programmes.* Syracuse, New York: Center for the Study of Teaching.

Argudín, V. Y. (2007). *Educación basada en competencias. Nociones y antecedentes*. Sevilla: Editorial MAD.

Bennet, N. (1979). *Estilos de enseñanza y progreso de los alumnos*. Madrid: Morata.

Blanco Blanco, A. (2007). Formación universitaria basada en competencias. In L. Prieto Navarro (Coord.), *La enseñanza universitaria centrada en el aprendizaje. Estrategias útiles para el profesorado* (pp. 31-59). Barcelona: Octaedro/ICE-UB.

Bueno, A., McLaren, N., & Madrid, D. (2005). Introduction: Second FL teacher education in the European context. In N. McLaren, D. Madrid, & A. Bueno (Eds.), *TEFL in Secondary Education* (pp. 23-41). Granada: Editorial Universidad de Granada.

CEF (2001). *Common European Framework of Reference for Language: Learning, Teaching, Assessment*. Strasbourg: Council of Europe.

Chappell, C. (1996). Quality and competence based education and training. *The Literacy Equation*, 71-79. Australia: Red Hill.

Consejo Educativo de Castilla y León (2007a). Aprendizaje por competencias: Un modelo a debatir. Retrieved from http://www.concejoeducativo.org/article.php?id_article=164, (01/01/13).

Consejo Educativo de Castilla y León (2007b). *Las competencias básicas en el currículo oficial: ¿Interés, peligro... o irrelevancia?* León: Concejo Educativo de Castilla-León.

Keteke, J. M. de, & Roesgiers, X. (1995). *Metodología para la recogida de información*. Madrid: La Muralla.

Gardner, H. (1983). *Frames of Mind: The Theory of Multiple Intelligences*. New York: Basic Books.

Gardner, H. (1999). *Intelligence Reframed: Multiple Intelligences for the 21st Century*. New York: Basic Books.

Gardner, H. (2001). *Las inteligencias múltiples hacia el siglo XXI*. Barcelona: Paidós.

Gimeno Sacristán, J. (2008). Diez tesis sobre la aparente utilidad de las competencias en educación. In J. Gimeno Sacristán *et al.* (Eds.), *Educar por competencias: ¿Qué hay de nuevo?* (pp. 15-58). Madrid: Morata.

Gimeno Sacristán, J., Pérez Gómez, A. I., Martínez, J. B., Torres, J., Angulo, F., & Álvarez, J. M. (2008). *Educar por competencias: ¿Qué hay de nuevo?* Madrid: Morata.

Goñi Zabala, J. M. (2007). *El espacio europeo de educación superior, un reto para la universidad. Competencias, tareas y evaluación, los ejes del currículo universitario*. Barcelona: Octaedro/ICE-UB.

Hipkins, R. (2006). *The Nature of the Key Competencies. A Background Paper*. New Zealand Council for Educational Research, New Zealand: Wellington.

Jacobs, G. M., & Farrell, T. S. C. (2001). Paradigm shift: Understanding and implementing change in second language education. *TESL-EJ*, *5*(1), 1-16. Retrieved from http://tesl-ej.org/ej17/a1.html (01/01/13).

Jiménez Benítez, J. R. (2006). Competencias básicas. *P@K-EN-REDES Revista Digital*, *1*(1), 1-8.

LOGSE (1990). Ley Orgánica General del Sistema Educativo español, Ley orgánica 1/1990, de 3 de octubre de 1990 (*Boletín Oficial del Estado*, 4 October).

Madrid, D. (1996). The FL teacher. In McLaren, N., & Madrid, D. (Eds.), *A Handbook for TEFL* (pp. 107-128). Alcoy: Marfil.

Madrid, D., & Hughes, S. (2009). The implementation of the European Credit Transfer System in initial foreign language teacher training. In M. L. Pérez Cañado (Ed.), *English Language in the European Credit Transfer System: Facing the Challenge* (pp. 227-244). Bern: Peter Lang.

Madrid, D., & Hughes, S. (2011). Competencies for foreign language teacher education. In M. L. Pérez Cañado (Ed.), *Competency-based Language Teaching in Higher Education.* Amsterdam: John Benjamins.

Madrid, D., & McLaren, N. (2004). Introduction to FL teacher education in the European context. In D. Madrid, & N. McLaren (Eds.), *EFL in Primary Education* (pp. 21-36). Granada: Editorial Universidad de Granada.

Moreno Moreno, P., & Soto Martínez, G. (2005). Una mirada reflexiva y crítica al enfoque por competencias. Educar, 73-80.

Pérez Gómez, A. I. (2007). *Las competencias básicas: Su naturaleza e implicaciones pedagógicas* (Cuaderno de Educación nº 1). Santander: Consejería de Educación de Cantabria.

Pérez González, J. (2009). Competencies in language teaching: From their conceptualisation to their concretion in the curriculum. In M. L. Pérez Cañado (Ed.), *English Language Teaching in the European Credit Transfer system: Facing the Challenge* (pp. 93-108). Bern: Peter Lang.

Rial Sánchez, A. (2007). Diseño curricular por competencias: El reto de la evaluación. In *Jornades d'avaluació dels aprenentatges a partir de competències*. Girona: La Universitat. Retrieved from http://hdl.handle.net/10256/819 (01/01/13).

Rychen, D. S., & Salganik, L. H. (Eds.) (2001). *Defining and Selecting Key Competences.* Gottingen: Hogrefe and Huber.

Rychen, D. S., & Salganik, L. H. (Eds.) (2003). *Key Competencies for a Successful Life and a Well-functioning Society*. Gottingen: Hogrefe and Huber.

Tobón, S. (2005). *Formación basada en competencias*. Bogotá: ECOE.

Torres Santomé, J. (2008). Obviando el debate sobre la cultura en el sistema educativo: Cómo ser competentes sin conocimientos. In J. Gimeno Sacristán *et al.* (Eds.), *Educar por competencias: ¿Qué hay de nuevo?* (pp. 143-175). Madrid: Morata.

UNESCO (1996). *La educación encierra un tesoro*. Paris: Ediciones UNESCO.

Vez, J. M. (2007). De políticas (y politiquillas) del EEES y competencias idiomáticas en el Grado de Maestro. *Lenguaje y Textos*, 25, 13-42.

A European Approach to Language Teaching: Developing Competency in the Usage of Web 2.0 Tools

Anna Franca Plastina

Abstract

This paper describes an experimental study carried out with the aim of preparing future EFL teachers for the lifelong process of competency development in e-Europe. A group of pre-service teachers (*N*=23) at the University of Calabria in Italy participated in Web 2.0 training, in which a European approach was adopted. A framework, grounded in European policy guidelines and training descriptors, was designed for experimental validity in the promotion of ICT-enhanced pedagogy. The non-formal context offered participants the opportunity to train in the usage of those Web 2.0 tools chosen to best respond to European recommendations in the key areas of language teaching improvement, professional development and innovation.

In the pre-training survey conducted, participants self-evaluated their digital competence at levels of core skills (Web 1.0 competence). Quantitative results from the post-training survey showed how participants achieved Web 2.0 competence, moving from the initial competence level of novices to the upper levels of practitioners. Qualitative findings were consistent with these results, reporting changes in participants' perception of their attitudes, knowledge and skills. The small-scale study attempts to contribute to narrowing the current European ICT-skills gap in local educational settings, where transformational guidance enables teachers to adopt a European approach to their praxis.

Introduction

Information and Communication Technology (ICT) remains a cross-cutting issue in the promotion of a current and future e-Europe. Over the last decade, the rapid development of the second-generation web, or Web 2.0 (O'Reilly, 2005; O'Reilly & Battelle, 2009) has had a transformative impact across all strata of society. Web 2.0 continues to play a catalytic role in democratizing dissemination of information and knowledge transfer with far-reaching implications. As these technological changes rapidly permeate all domains of the European society, a Digital Agenda for Europe (European Commission, 2010) has been set up to sensitize stakeholders to monitor technological progress and assess subsequent challenges. The Agenda points out how "Europe is suffering from a growing professional ICT skills shortage and a digital literacy deficit, [which] are excluding many citizens from the digital society and economy [...] (2010: 6). Thus, the action of reducing the ICT-skills gap appears to be one of the biggest challenges to modernize 21st-century Europe. In other words, external technological developments determine social exclusion caused by skills obsolescence (Grip *et al.*, 2002), and by differences in the extent and ways in which technology is used in different societal domains, among European state members, and between Europe and other more technologically-advanced countries.

In particular, the challenge of narrowing this gap appears to strongly affect the domain of education, where the impact of ICT on learning processes relies on the extent to which teachers use educational technology. Egbert *et al.* (2002) underscore the importance of having pre- and in-service language teachers learn about computer use. However, Balanskat (2005: 11) warns that "how far teachers can cope with the new demands depends a lot on their ability to become learners themselves again and engage in a life long learning process", and suggests that "policies need to tackle both in the future the objectives as well as the concrete means for implementation". Enhancing ICT training in decentralised contexts of teacher education becomes extremely important to understand how current technological innovations can properly position local pedagogical praxis within the wider European context. The effective use of educational technology demands a paradigm shift from the traditional model of teaching towards ICT-enhanced pedagogy, which summons teachers to question their traditional roles. For this reason, neglecting technology as an educational resource means that teachers run the risk of educating learners to acquire obsolescent skills, which contribute to their exclusion from the current and future knowledge-based society. Smerdon *et al.* (2000) have found, in fact, that teachers mostly use the computer to support their traditional practice, and that even more experienced teachers limit their use to word processing and spreadsheets, and to some extent to Internet research. It is therefore important to develop teachers' perception of the usefulness of ICT for teaching through hands-on experiences, in which they are encouraged to overcome technology-related anxiety (Knezek *et al.*, 1996). A helpful support in this direction can be provided by surveys of teachers' attitudes, knowledge and skills.

This paper describes an experimental study which was carried out with the aim of enhancing the usage of Web 2.0 tools in language teacher education. The study specifically attempted to promote technological innovation in pre-service training, and adopted a European approach to overcome constraints related to training in local contexts. For this purpose, the design and implementation of the experiment were grounded in a framework based on European policies and documents. In the first part of the paper, the concepts of competence and competency are introduced in order to discuss the challenges which arise with digital competence in the field of education. In this perspective, the importance of adopting a European stance to language teacher education is highlighted through the support of the most relevant European policies and recommendations on the issue. The experimental study, which is presented as the core of the paper, is set against this scenario.

1 Technology: A bridge or a barrier?

The interchangeable use of competence and competency may lead to considerable misunderstanding of the difference between the two terms. Rowe (1995) explains that competence refers to a skill and the standard of performance, whereas competency concerns the behaviour by which the skill is achieved. The lifelong process of competency development therefore entails *doing and reflecting* to acquire different levels of competence. The model introduced by Dreyfus & Dreyfus (1980) provides support in understanding that different levels of competence are entailed in competency development. In particular, the model proposes five levels of competence through which competency can be achieved: 1. *novice* or rule-based behaviour, which is strongly limited and inflexible; 2. *experienced beginner*, who incorporates aspects of the situation; 3. *practitioner*, who acts consciously with long-term goals and plans; 4. *knowledgeable practitioner*, who has a holistic view of the situation and whose action relies on personal conviction; 5. *expert*, who has an intuitive understanding of the situation and its central aspects.

From a European point of view, competence is defined as the "ability to apply knowledge, know-how and skills in a habitual or changing situation" (Tissot, 2004). This implies adopting the lifelong learning paradigm of competency development continuously to acquire knowledge, skills and new capabilities. Among the key competences for lifelong learning, the European Commission (2004) emphasises the importance of achieving digital competence, or the confident and critical use of electronic media for work, leisure and communication. However, in the field of education, challenges arise in adapting to ICT-enhanced pedagogy due to the generation gap between teachers and learners. On the one hand, learners have spent most of their lives surrounded by, and multitasking with computers, video games, cellular phones, digital cameras, digital music players, and the Internet (Lehnart *et al.*, 2005). They therefore want and expect to have learning material in multiple media, and opportunities to interact online with peers (Levin & Arafeh, 2002). On the other hand, teachers are still more at ease in the world of books, newspapers, and other traditional media. They therefore tend to use technology in ways that fit their current practice. According to Prensky (2001: 1-2):

> by virtue of being born in the digital age, our students are *Digital Natives* by definition [...]. Those of us who were not born into the digital world are [...] *Digital Immigrants*. As Digital Immigrants learn – like all immigrants, some better than others – to adapt to their environment, they always retain, to some degree, their "accent", that is, their foot in the past. [...] *our Digital Immigrant instructors, who speak an*

outdated language (that of the pre-digital age), are struggling to teach a population that speaks an entirely new language [original emphasis].

Prensky (2010: 5) futher points out that "while there is much about the future that we don't know, we know enough to understand that today's English students must be posting, publishing, and communicating with the world in the multiple media of today and tomorrow". Thus, teachers need to come to grips with the issue of preparing their learners to become skilled citizens of the future. They should realise that acquiring digital competence also involves other important competences such as logical and critical thinking, high-level information management skills, and well-developed communication skills (European Commission (2004: 7).

One way of bridging the ICT gap can be through training programmes, which guide teachers to adopt a transformational perspective of technology while training in the effective use of digital tools. This implies gaining understanding of the current paradigm shift of teaching from a process of knowledge transmission towards enhancing the lifelong process of competency development. Research studies have shown that learning mediated by technology is more effective than the knowledge-transmission modality of instruction (Johnson & Johnson, 1996). However, teachers appear to struggle in making transformational changes to develop their *technofluency*, as they still receive little support of any kind. Lund (2004: 30-31) points out how "for teachers, it is important that they take part in such emerging practices. How can a teacher teach something he/she has not herself come to understand and practice?". This question may well be directed to those institutions which still underestimate that "the current technological paradigm shift, whereby *fixed* knowledge in fixed time and fixed place has constantly developed into accessible anytime/anyplace knowledge, offers an extraordinarily innovative change […]" (Plastina, 2007: 235). Re-training in-service teachers and preparing pre-service teachers for their future entry into the educational system lies at the forefront of language teacher education.

1.1 Europeanising language teacher education

Over the last decade, different official European institutions have intensively promoted policies on the integration of ICT in language teaching and learning. The Final Report on *The Impact of Information and Communications Technologies on the Teaching of Foreign Languages and on the Role of Teachers of Foreign Languages* (Directorate General of Education and Culture, 2002: 4-5) points out that:

> *Teacher training* is shown to be *the key* to the successful introduction and deployment of the new media. [...] With regard to pedagogy and methodology, research has shown that a *'shift of paradigm' is necessary in teacher/learner roles.* [...] *language teachers* are the most *open to* the use of *the new media*. However, *the use and deployment of ICT in FLT and FLL is far from satisfactory* [...] [original emphasis].

In this view, the *Action Plan 2004-2006*, issued by the European Commission (2003), can be considered a milestone in promoting a policy of language learning and linguistic diversity. In targeting the three key areas of promoting lifelong learning, improving language teaching, and creating a more language-friendly environment, the Plan has had a significant impact at both top-down and bottom-up levels. In the latter case, it has led to the creation of the European Profile for Language Teacher Education (EPLTE) – A Frame of Reference (Kelly *et al.*, 2004), which is designed to cater for language teacher education in 21st-century Europe. Empirical data have also been collected through different policy-analysis surveys to pinpoint those areas in need of priority. Through surveys of teachers' ICT competence, Balanskat (2005) found that ICT monitoring is extremely necessary also in the area of teacher training with specific focus on competencies.

On the other hand, central policies have also been affected by the Action Plan. In particular, the *Recommendation of the European Parliament and the Council of Europe* (2006) targets eight key competences for lifelong learning. Of these, three are particularly relevant for language teaching and learning: communication in foreign languages, digital competence, and learning to learn. In this direction, the European Education, Audiovisual and Culture Executive Agency (EACEA) commissioned *The Study on the Impact of Information and Communications Technology (ICT) and New Media on Language Learning* (EACEA, 2007/2009). The Final Report (Ellinogermaniki Agogi, 2009) stresses how traditional teaching/learning paradigms are becoming obsolete in preparing the digital citizens of *e-Europe*. Recommendations are therefore specified for the key area of Professional Development. Furthermore, the report emphasises the importance of context-driven instruction for ICT competency in language learning. The issued recommendations are not only targeted to formal learning contexts, where traditional teacher-learner relationships take place. They broaden the field of vision to encompass *non-formal* learning, which may occur outside the formal system and *informal* learning, based on experiential learning from our daily lives (cf. European Commission, 2000).

While these central policies cast the foundations for a European dimension of language teacher education, research studies show that traditional instruction models are still replicated by teacher training institutions (e.g. Hauge, 2003). At grassroot levels, digital competency appears to lag behind the recommendations issued by European policies. Rasmussen & Ludvigsen (2009) argue that negotiations between policies, models, and practices need to be stipulated. To this end, a consortium of European institutions has been established to provide insights and offer solutions for the optimisation of language teacher training in Europe (Ziegler *et al.*, 2009). At the same time, small-scale experiments have been reported (Redecker *et al.*, 2009) on the use of ICT in different European institutions for different educational purposes. The experimental study reported below is a contribution in this sense.

2 The experimental study: Design and method

Experimental design relied on two main European documents: 1. the Final Report on The Study on the Impact of Information and Communications Technology (ICT) and New Media on Language Learning (Ellinogermaniki Agogi, 2009); 2. the European Profile for Language Teacher Education (EPLTE) – A Frame of Reference (Kelly *et al.*, 2004). These documents were chosen for three main reasons. First, central policies have still not specified the goals for the development of teachers' digital competency. While the European policy guidelines recommended in the Final Report helped frame the experiment in general terms, the training descriptors included in the EPLTE were specifically targeted to language teachers and to their competency development. Second, the integrated use of these documents supported a holistic European approach to the experiment, based on the combination of top-down and bottom-up views of language teacher education. In turn, this approach was adopted to ensure that the experiment carried out at the local level conveyed a European dimension of training. Third, the guidelines and descriptors were introduced to account for experimental validity and reliability.

2.1 Participants

Twenty-three pre-service teachers (19 females; 4 males), whose age ranged from 25 to 30 years (M=26), participated in the small-scale experiment. All participants were attending the last semester of their two-year training course at the Teacher College of the University of Calabria in southern Italy. After a final exam, they would qualify as English language teachers, and enter the Italian education system. As in many European institutions, ICT training was not offered by their institutional course of studies. Participants were therefore willing to take advantage of undergoing experimental training.

2.2 Training tools

Web 2.0 tools were chosen for the experiment, as they were considered to best respond to the two European recommendations of promoting innovation and professional development. In terms of innovation, Web 2.0 tools (e.g. blogs, wikis, podcasts, social networking) are emerging practices, which have a cross-cutting impact on all societal domains. Compared to the static feature of first-generation applications, Web 2.0 tools are highly innovative, as their dynamic functionalities have revolutionised the communicative modality of interacting, sharing and collaborating *anytime anywhere* through the *Read/Write* Web.

In terms of professional development, Web 2.0 tools have a potential in facilitating learner-centred approaches, whereas static Web 1.0 tools expose the weakness of supporting teacher-centred practices. Moreover, Web 2.0 multimodal functionalities enable collaborative authorship and readership, support lifelong learning, and are cost-effective. Blogger.com and Wordle.net were the Web 2.0 tools used for training. The first tool was chosen for its socially-transformative democratizing potential (Herring *et al.*, 2004) of journal writing. In teacher education, journal writing has been found to be a core component of reflective teacher development (e.g. Gebhard, 1999; Plastina, 2006). A collaborative *journal* blog was considered suitable for professional development, which encourages learner autonomy (Little, 1999). The tool offered participants "concrete opportunities to form their own community in which they engage in collaborative learning processes leading to innovative teaching practices" (Plastina, 2009: 40). Collaborative authorship and readership support logical and critical thinking, and enhance the lifelong learning skills of *doing and reflecting*. The use of this Web 2.0 tool was also considered important for ICT-enhanced pedagogy, as its popularity "outside the foreign language classroom may be a motivating force for technologically savvy young learners" (Pinkman, 2005: 14). Finally, its open-source environment well responded to European recommendations on non-formal learning contexts, which could determine positive changes in participants' perception of Web 2.0 (cf. Plastina, 2010).

Wordle.net was the other tool used for training. Its innovative ease of use and creative functionality were considered important in building Web 2.0 confidence, and in overcoming technology-related anxiety. The tool is purposed to generate *wordles* (word clouds), in which different word sizes depend on their frequency rate in the source text. These can be any pasted text or entered URL. *Wordles* can be customized in font, colour, shape and size, supporting motivation and creativity. *Wordles* further encourage the development of information processing skills, underlying critical thinking and self-reflection. They also enhance awareness-raising of how Web 2.0 can be integrated in different language activities such as brainstorming and word association, as well as being compatible with blog embedment.

2.3 Procedure

Experimental training was carried out in four main phases: 1. survey of participants' pre-training digital competence; 2. experimental Web 2.0 practice; 3. survey of participants' post-training Web 2.0 competence; 4. data analysis.

In the first phase, participants' digital competence was diagnosed using a checklist designed for self-evaluation. Participants were asked to rate their digital competence on a four-point scale ranging from 1 (no competence) to 4 (yes-fully competent). The 15 items were designed to include three levels of skills: core, advanced, specialist.

In the second phase, objectives were set using a framework based on European policy guidelines and teacher education descriptors. Instructions on the purpose of the experiment and on its modality of non-formal learning were then provided. However, the eight-week training experiment was blended with the institutional module participants were attending with the same teacher educator for content discussions. At the end of this phase, participants were required to create wordles of short self-reflective texts about the experience.

In the third phase, when experimental training was over, participants' Web 2.0 competence was surveyed. A 15-item questionnaire was used for the purpose. Its design was based on the Framework for Key Competences in a Knowledge-Based Society (European Commission, 2004), which entails attitudes, knowledge and skills as key components of competence. Participants rated items on a five-point Likert scale ranging from 1 – strongly disagree to 5 – strongly agree.

In the fourth and final phase, quantitative analysis of survey data was conducted and qualitative analysis of wordles was then carried out.

3 A European approach to web 2.0 training

A framework was designed for the experiment, based on recommendations on professional development (EACEA, 2007/2009) and on indicators of language teaching improvement (EPLTE).

In detail, the framework included one particular recommendation on professional development in new systems, and its three procedural policy guidelines. It also encompassed four training descriptors taken from the 40 elements presented in the EPLTE, which served as both a guideline to design the experiment, and as a checklist for its effectiveness. Each descriptor was chosen to cover the four

EPLTE key areas: *structure*, *knowledge and understanding*, *strategies and skills*, and *value*. In this way, the framework facilitated the adoption of a European approach to pre-service training, and supported experimental validity and reliability. European policy guidelines and descriptors included in the framework are illustrated in Table 1 below.

Table 1: The framework for Web 2.0 training using a European approach

European Policy Guidelines *(EACEA 2007/2009 Report)*	**European Descriptors** *(EPLTE, 2004)*
Create opportunities for teachers to learn, practise and develop confidence in new systems through:	1. *Structure* Organize participation in ICT learning environments;
1. Opportunities for experimentation, rehearsal and practice with new technologies by creating virtual learning environments;	2. *Knowledge & Understanding* Train in ICT for resource discovery, and pedagogical use in the language classroom;
2. Learning via experiential tasks within a personal, confidential and non-threatening environment;	3. *Strategies & Skills* Train in methods of learning to learn;
3. Inculcating confidence in professional language educators in ICT use and application.	4. *Values* Train in the importance of lifelong learning.

A journal blog[1] was set up as a safe environment by activating the function of restricting authorship and readership access only to group members (see Table 1: policy guidelines 1 & 2; EPLTE descriptor 1). Discussion questions related to formal course content were posted each week as experiential tasks. Participants were then given the opportunity to organise and regulate their own learning in the Web 2.0 environment (EPLTE descriptors 2 and 3). After writing short self-reflective texts on their experience, participants created and shared their *wordles* (policy guideline 3; EPLTE descriptor 4).

The framework therefore set the following levels of competence, which the pre-service teachers were trained to acquire:

- know and understand about innovative Web 2.0 tools as new professional resources;

1 http://ssissunicalblog.blogspot.com.

- use collaborative strategies to develop processes of learning to learn in order to acquire new Web 2.0 skills;
- engage in self- and collaborative reflective processes which enhance awareness of the value of the digital competence acquired.

4 Findings

Both quantitative and qualitative data findings are reported in this section. Pre- and post survey results are discussed in the following section, while qualitative findings on wordles are presented in section 4.2.

4.1 Quantitative findings

All participants self-evaluated their digital competence prior to experimental training. Raw data were manipulated for frequency of occurrence of participants' ratings. Survey findings indicate how a high number of participants (*N*=20-23) evaluated themselves as fully competent at the *core* level of digital skills. Ratings decreased significantly for *advanced* skills, showing a competency-gap between Web 1.0 (core skills) and Web 2.0 competences (*N*=5-23). However, these figures also reveal how participants (*N*=4-12) were positive about the possibility of developing Web 2.0 competency if they were offered support. Ratings dramatically dropped to no competence in most *specialist* Web 2.0 skills (*N*=21-23). Overall, the pre-training survey diagnosed that participants needed to engage in developing digital-competency at advanced and specialist levels, which corresponded to Web 2.0 usage.

Self-ratings of prior digital competence are shown in Table 2. Figures refer to frequency of occurrence per number of participants and per level of digital competence. Overall, findings indicate that participants' competency development was at a standstill. While they were found to be *experts* at core skills, they were *novices* at upper levels of digital competence (cfr. Dreyfus & Dreyfus, 1980). The challenge, which experimental training was required to cope with, was to help them upgrade their competency development through the acquisition of new levels of competence.

Table 2: Prior digital competence: Self-ratings per number of participants and levels

Levels of Digital Competence	Frequency of Occurrence of Participants' Ratings ($N = 23$)			
	Scale of Ratings			
	No	Yes with help	Yes – mostly competent	Yes - fully competent
Core Skills				
1. Enter a known web address to access a site	--	--	--	23
2. Use a search engine to find information	--	--	--	23
3. Add useful sites to Favourites to visit again	--	--	--	23
4. Cut and paste texts	--	--	2	21
5. Save a web page	--	--	3	20
Advanced Skills				
1.Subscribe to a blog	14	4	3	2
2.Create a blog account	12	5	2	2
3.Customize layouts	5	12	4	2
4.Upload images	11	10	--	2
5.Use screencasting software	23	--	--	--
Specialist Skills				
1. Create Wordles	23	--	--	--
2. Upload videos	2	19	--	2
3. Add feed readers (RSS)	23	--	--	--
4. Download and install plug-ins	21	--	--	1
5. Embed Wordles in blogs	23	--	--	--

The post-training survey invited participants to self-rate their digital competence in terms of attitudes, knowledge and skills, based on the training received. Ratings were performed on a five-point Likert scale: strongly disagree (SD), disagree (D), neither agree nor disagree (N), agree (A) or strongly agree (SA). Findings show how participants' perception of their attitudes to Web 2.0 was positive (strongly agree: 16-23; agree: 2-7). These results indicate how the experience was beneficial for their confidence, willingness, motivation, and awareness of Web 2.0 usage, which ultimately stimulated their positive attitude to the usefulness of digital tools in their future classrooms. The group of pre-service teachers also perceived their acquisition of new knowledge related to pedagogical changes, reflective processes, collaborative learning, and creativity (strongly agree: 17-23; agree: 3-5), understanding how these can support new learning practices. Moreover, skills development related to the usage of blogs and wordles was perceived even more positively by all participants (strongly agree: 23), who were eventually skilled in simulating the integration of Web 2.0 in some language activities, as reported in Table 3 below.

Table 3: Participants' perception of their post-training Web 2.0 competence

Digital Competence Levels for Competency-Development (***Attitudes, knowledge and skills***)	**SA**	**A**	**N**	**D**	**SD**
A. Attitudes - I now feel:					
- more confident in using Web 2.0 tools	21	2	=	=	=
- more willing to take responsibility for my learning	16	7	=	=	=
- more motivated to collaborate with peers	23	=	=	=	=
- more conscious of Web 2.0 integration in L2 classrooms	18	5	=	=	=
- more stimulated in their pedagogical use	19	4	=	=	=
B. Knowledge - I now know that Web 2.0 learning can:					
- change from classroom learning	23	=	=	=	=
- support self-reflection	23	=	=	=	=
- encourage peer collaboration	23	=	=	=	=
- stimulate creativity	20	3	=	=	=
- support my future teaching praxis	17	5	=	=	=
C. Skills - I now can:					
- create a blog account	23	=	=	=	=
- write & edit postings, and comments	23	=	=	=	=
- upload images; add RSS feeds	23	=	=	=	=
- create wordles	23	=	=	=	=
- simulate the use of these in some language activities	23	=	=	=	=

4.2. Qualitative findings

Participants' self-reflective texts and relative *wordles* were also analyzed to understand *how* they perceived their development of Web 2.0 competency. Qualitative patterns of *changes* were identified and classified under the categories of attitudes, understanding, knowledge, strategies, skills and values. Significant sample texts and *wordles* are presented for each category in Figures 1-6 below.

- Changing attitudes

An extremely positive attitude towards the experimental training experience was manifested through the enduring willingness to engage in a new learning environment, which was eventually found to be more motivating than the traditional classroom.

As one participant reflected: *Books, photocopies, worksheets, lesson plans, modules have been* **haunting** *and haunting our days since the training experience started. Then came blogs... It was first hard to enter this blog and understand it, but then I discovered a new world where I had fun, fun and more fun in learning so much* (Daniela).

Haunting and *Fun* are the contrasting keywords highlighted in the related wordle in Figure 1 on changing attitudes.

Fig. 1: Wordle on Changing Attitudes: From being haunted to having fun

- Developing understanding

Changes were also witnessed in participants' increased understanding of how the new learning environment drammatically altered teacher/learner roles compared to those in the traditional classroom.

On this issue, one trainee declared: *It is strange how we can easily change our perspective of people: our teacher no longer seems to me a person training us as future teachers. She's not a teacher anymore, but a real HELPFUL FRIEND in cyberspace for us LEARNERS: alias a BLOGGATOR who has guided us through the storm, talking and listening to US* (Letizia).

As in the wordle represented in Figure 2, *Learners* understand that the role enacted by the teacher in *Cyberspace* is that of being a *helpful person, a friend*, who is informally defined as a *Bloggator*.

Fig. 2: Wordle on understanding: Changes in teacher/learner roles

- Acquiring knowledge

The knowledge acquired about the differences between Web 1.0 and Web 2.0 also had some hilarious outcomes in real-world contexts as witnessed by one trainee:

The lady at the reception in the National Library scolded me because she thought I was writing e-mails which are forbidden. I tried explaining that 'blogging' is different from writing e-mails...but she ignores what a BLOG is! (Rosanna).

The wordle in Figure 3 indicates how there is a gap between the trainee's acquired knowledge related to the keyword *blog* and the lady's restricted knowledge related to the keyword *emails*.

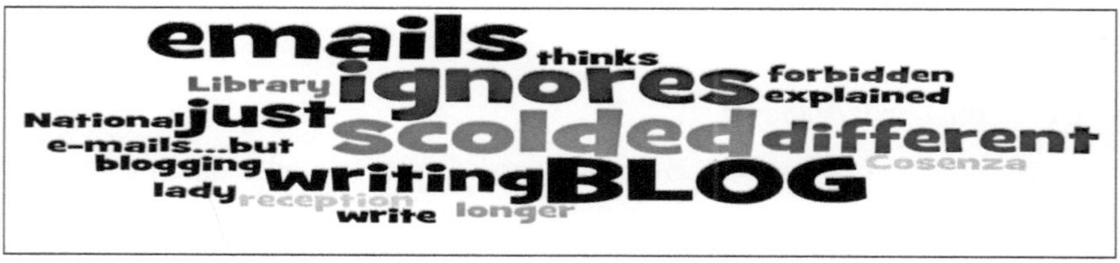

Fig. 3: Wordle on knowledge: Differences between Web 1.0 and 2.0

- Developing strategies

Participants also realised that they inevitably developed strategies to cope with the different problems encountered in the new learning environment. In this regard, one trainee pointed out how she took responsibility for her own learning:

I feel l worked so hard to make this tool work for me. I had trouble understanding how the thing worked sometimes. My intuition and a bit of logic gave me the strength to manage. Blogging is gr8! (Angela)

Thus, the strategies of *intuition* and *logic* were at the forefront of changes in this trainee's experience of coping with difficulties, as shown in Figure 4.

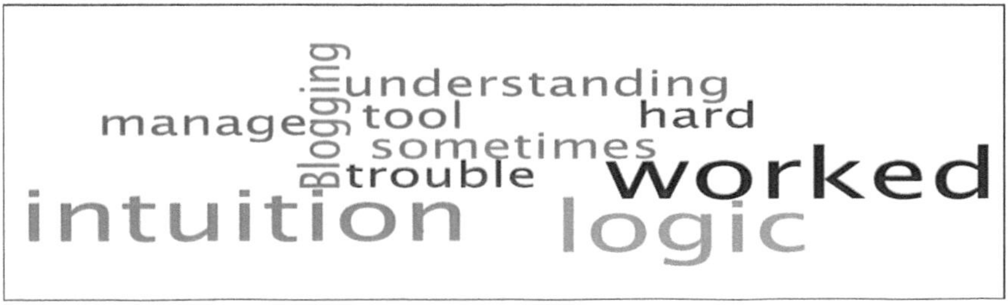

Fig. 4: *Wordle on strategies: Overcoming difficulties*

- Developing skills

Positive attitudes were also shown through self-reflections on how skills were better developed in the new learning environment.

As an example, one participant stated: *THANK YOU for letting me learn to become skilled in Web 2.0. I have become a critical thinker while I enjoyed developing digital skills in this fantastic way of training (Nadia).*

This reflection is shown in Figure 5, where the keywords *thinker*, *skills* and *skilled* on the left side of the wordle can be seen as the outcome of the keywords *training* and *become* on the right side.

Fig. 5: *Wordle on skills: Digital and critical thinking*

- Web 2.0 value

Changes regarding the value attributed to Web 2.0 were witnessed by participants' reflections on the benefit that language pedagogy can draw from this resource.

As one trainee reflected: *Web 2.0 (Blogging & Wordling) is an interesting approach to motivate, inspire, promote our future students' language learning. They love the web so why stick only to textbooks? Don't complain if you bore your students with outdated tools. Let's face it: weaker students can get help from the others, and unmotivated ones enjoy the fun* (Giuseppe).

Web and *Students* are the keywords highlighted in the wordle in Figure 6, which shows how Web 2.0 was valued following the experimental training experience.

5 Concluding remarks

ICT tools are still in their embryonic phase of deployment in European institutional Education and Training (Redecker *et al.*, 2009). As a consequence, research studies have not yet provided sufficient scientific evidence on their impact in these areas. Education systems throughout Europe have not been, in fact, willing so far to move away from the traditional paradigm based on the transfer of knowledge from teacher to student (European Commission, 2008). As a result, all too often foreign language teachers are not completely aware of technological developments, and are therefore unable or unwilling to implement changes in their teaching praxis (EACEA, 2007/2009).

At institutional levels, policy makers are summoned to promote innovation in teacher education, and to contribute to the modernisation of European education systems in accordance with the Lisbon strategy. Based on these assumptions, the present experimental study has attempted to promote the opportunity of implementing pre-service teacher training grounded in a European approach to enhance professional development and innovation. Key policies and guidelines were used as the framework for training in the usage of Web 2.0 tools. Survey findings showed how significant changes occurred. In the pre-training stage, participants' competence was rated at the core level of Web 1.0, and at the *novice* level of Web 2.0 competence. In the post-training stage, pre-service teachers perceived their attitudes, knowledge and skills differently, moving to the upper competence level of *practitioners.* The experiment further showed how training in ICT does not mean placing focus merely on the development of technical competence in using specific digital tools. It rather indicates that participants were engaged in ongoing reflection first related to resource discovery and application, and then based on the pedagogical value of Web 2.0 integration in the language classroom.

In sum, teacher education in a European dimension is a key factor in responding to the ICT-skills gap, which challenges 21st-century Europe. In decentralised contexts where traditional practices are hard to eradicate and where the risk of training in obsolete skills is real, teacher education plays a crucial role in bringing professional development to the wider European context of social innovation. Competency training must therefore sensitize trainees to develop levels of competence in which *learning to use* gives way to *using to learn*.

Bibliography

Balanskat, A. (2005). Assessment schemes for teachers' ICT competence - A policy analysis. Results from PIC/P2P survey, INSIGHT: Observatory for new technologies and education. European Schoolnet.

Directorate General of Education and Culture (2002). *The Impact of Information and Communications Technologies on the Teaching of Foreign Languages and on the Role of Teachers of Foreign Languages*. Brussels.

Dreyfus, S., & Dreyfus, H. (1980). *A Five-Stage Model of the Mental Activities Involved in Directed Skill Acquisition*. Washington, DC: Storming Media.

Egbert, J., Paulus, T., & Nakamichi, Y. (2002). The impact of CALL instruction on classroom computer use: A foundation for rethinking technology in teacher education. *Language Learning & Technology*, *6*(3), 108-126.

Ellinogermaniki Agogi (2009). Final Report: *The Study on the Impact of Information and Communications Technology (ICT) and New Media on Language Learning (2007/2009)*, Brussels: EACEA.

European Commission (2000). *A Memorandum on Lifelong Learning*. 30.10.2000.SEC (2000) 1832, Brussels.

European Commission (2003). *Action Plan "Promoting Language Learning and Linguistics Diversity" (2004-2006)*. 24.07.2003. COM (2003) 499 final, Brussels.

European Commission (2004). Implementation of "Education and Training 2010" Work Programme. Working Group B "Key Competences". *Key Competences for Lifelong Learning a European Reference Framework*. Brussels.

European Commission (2008). *Proposal for a Decision of the European Parliament and of the Council concerning the European Year of Creativity and Innovation (2009)*, COM (2008) 159 final, Brussels.

European Commission (2010). *A Digital Agenda for Europe*, COM (2010) 245, Brussels.

Gebhard, J. G. (1999). Reflecting through a teaching journal. In J. G. Gebhard, & R. Oprandy (Eds.), *Language Teaching Awareness: A Guide to Exploring Beliefs and Practices* (pp. 78-98). Cambridge: Cambridge University Press.

Grip, A. de, Loo van, J., & Mayhew, K. (Eds.). (2002). The economics of skills obsolescence: Theoretical innovations and empirical applications. *Research in Labor Economics, 21*. Amsterdam, Elsevier.

Hauge, T. E. (2003). *Praktisk pedagogigisk utdanning i digitale læringsomgivelser. Sluttrapport fra PLUTO prosjektet 2000-2003*, ITU, pp. 1-33.

Herring, S., Scheidt, L., Bonus, S., & Wright, E. (2004). Bridging the gap: A genre analysis of weblogs. In *Proceedings of the Thirty-seventh Hawaii International Conference on System Sciences (HICSS-37)*. Los Alamitos: IEEE Press.

Johnson, D., & Johnson, R. (1996). Cooperation and the use of technology. In D. H. Jonassen (Ed.), *Handbook of Research for Educational Communications and Technology* (pp. 1017-1044). New York: Simon & Schuster.

Kelly, M., Grenfell, M., Allan, R., Kriza, C., & McEvoy, W. (2004). *European Profile for Language Teacher Education: A Frame of Reference*. Southampton: University of Southampton, European Commission Directorate General for Education and Culture.

Knezek, G., Chiristensen, R., & Rice, D. (1996). Changes in teacher attitudes during information technology training. *Technology and Teacher Education Annual, 6*, 763-766.

Lehnart, A., Madden, M. & Hitlin, P. (2005). *Teens and Technology*. Washington, DC: PEW Internet & American Life Project.

Levin, D., & Arafeh, S. (2002). *The Digital Disconnect: The Widening Gap between Internetsavvy Students and Their Schools*. Washington, DC: Pew Internet & American Life Project.

Little, D. (1999). Freedom to learner and compulsion to interact: Promoting learner autonomy through the use of information systems and information technologies. In R. Pemberton, E. S. L. Li, W. W. F. Or & H. D. Pierson (Eds.), *Taking Control: Autonomy in Language Learning* (pp. 203-218). Hong Kong: Hong Kong University Press.

Lund, A. (2004). Teachers as agents of change: ICTs and a reconsideration of teacher expertise. In *Information and Communication Technologies in the Teaching and Learning of Foreign Languages: State-of-the-Art, Needs and Perspectives* (pp. 27-37). Moscow: UNESCO Institute.

O'Reilly, T. (2005). *What is Web 2.0*. O'Reilly Network. Retrieved from www.oreillynet.com/pub/a/oreilly/tim/news/2005/09/30/what-is-web-20.html (01/01/13).

O'Reilly, T., & Battelle, J. (2009). *Web Squared: Web 2.0 Five Years On*. Retrieved from http://assets.en.oreilly.com/1/event/28/web2009_websquared-whitepaper.pdf (01/01/13).

Pinkman, K. (2005). Using blogs in the foreign language classroom: Encouraging learner independence. *The JALT CALL Journal, 1*(1), 12-24.

Plastina, A. F. (2006). Meeting CEF standards: Research action in local action research. In S. Borg (Ed.), *Language Teacher Research in Europe*, *Language Teacher Research Series* (T. Farrell, Ed.) (pp. 95-107). Alexandria, Va: TESOL Publications.

Plastina, A. F. (2007). Towards a digital perspective of European languages: Designing and producing an EFL learning object. In R. Laugier (Ed.), *Le Lingue Europee in Prospettiva* (pp. 235-252). Soveria Mannelli: Rubbettino.

Plastina, A. F. (2009). Nurturing communities of practice: The case of a TESOL VCoP in Italy. In K. Cadman, J. Barnett, & C. Guerin (Eds.), *TESOL in Context, Special Edition S2 'Pedagogies of Connection'* (pp. 40-52).

Plastina, A. F. (2010). The language of academic weblogs: How personality is projected and perceived. In L. Scliar-Cabral (Ed.), *Psycholinguistics: Scientific and Technological Challenges* (pp. 350-363). Porto Alegre: Editora Universitària da PUCR.

Prensky, M. (2001). Digital natives, digital immigrants. *On the Horizon, 9*(5), 1-6.

Prensky, M. (2010). *Teaching Digital Natives: Partnering for Real Learning*. Thousand Oaks: Corwin.

Rasmussen, I., & Ludvigsen, S. (2009). The hedgehog and the fox: A discussion of the approaches to the analysis of ICT reforms in teacher education of Larry Cuban and Yrjö Engeström. *Mind, Culture, and Activity, 16*, 83-104.

Recommendation of the European Parliament and of the Council (2006). Key competences for lifelong learning (2006/962/EC). *Official Journal of the European Union*, L 394 of 30.12.

Redecker, C., Ala-Mutka, K., Bacigalupo, M., Ferrari, A, & Punie, Y. (2009). *Learning 2.0: The Impact of Web 2.0 Innovations on Education and Training in Europe*. Luxembourg: Office for Official Publications of the European Communities.

Rowe, C. (1995). Clarifying the use of competence and competency models in recruitment, assessment and staff development. *Industrial and Commercial Training 27*(11), 12-17. MCB University Press.

Smerdon, B., Cronen, S., Lanahan, L., Anderson, J., Iannotti, N., & Angeles, J. (2000). *Teachers' Tools for the 21st Century: A Report on Teachers' Use of Technology*. Washington, DC: National Center for Education Statistics.

Tissot, P. (2004). *Terminology of Vocational Training Policy: A Multilingual Glossary for an Enlarged Europe*. Luxembourg: Office for Official Publications of the European Communities.

Ziegler, G., Eskildsen, L., Bottin, C., & Coonan, M. C. (2009). *Training Teachers of Languages in Europe, Analytic Report*. Paris/Bruxelles: SEMLANG.

What's HappeNING?
Expanding the ESL Classroom through Educational Social Network Sites

Anna María Brígido-Corachán & María Goretti Zaragoza-Ninet

Abstract

In this case study we analyze the impact of the educational social network site NING on an upper-level ESL module at the University of Valencia, Spain. We discuss the didactic advantages provided by this multimodal online tool that integrates digital literacies with the creative practice of writing, reading and listening activities in the English language. Our students managed personal profiles, wrote blog entries, frequently discussed self-produced photos and videos, completed grammar and vocabulary exercises, and opened forum discussions where heated debates regularly coexisted with the sharing of meaningful personal and academic information and peer-advice. These multidirectional dialogues fostered the creation of a community of support that strengthened self-managed linguistic practice, student motivation and confidence. Our results show that the use of this educational platform greatly improved our students' digital, communicative and collaborative skills, bringing ESL learning to a whole new level.

Introduction: Generation 2.0. enters the university classroom

Teachers and scholars around the world agree that university educators need to rethink their pedagogical models for ESL learning and embrace student-centered methodologies, collaborative practices, Information and Cummunication Technology (ICT) tools, and multiliteracies in adult/tertiary education (Bartlett-Bragg, 2006; Pennock, 2009; Pasadas Ureña, 2010; Pérez Cañado, 2009; Warshauer & Kern, 2000). Learning should no longer be constrained by the physical walls of the classroom nor be exclusively guided by a lecturing instructor/authority. According to Anne Bartlett-Bragg, informal adult learning can spring from social interactions when a motivated learner observes and consciously or unconsciously imitates his/her peers' social and linguistic behavior (2007: 2). Even in traditional university settings, students have always been exposed to non-teacher mediated learning opportunities and often create their own "communities of practice" (Bartlett-Bragg, 2006: 8) at the university cafeteria, at the library or at the study hall. These informal, peer-to-peer learning exchanges have recently undergone an explosion as Web 2.0. platforms and applications such as social networks, blogs, and chats, among others, infiltrate our daily habits. Informal learning activities carried out using computer-mediated communication (CMC) include networking, mentoring, learning from advisors, problem-solving, Internet searches, information distribution, self-analysis and critical reflection (Bartlett-Bragg, 2006: 3). These are all autonomous and collaborative learning skills that are widely promoted in the new European Higher Education Area (EHEA) context. They are, however, not always successfully integrated with face-to-face tuition nor assessed as part of the students' final grade.

Younger generations in Spain have a *connective* approach to the world, what Francisco Yus (2010) refers to as "being in the network" [*estar en la red*]. Indeed, new youth cultures all over the world are more than ever *relational* and express themselves through a physical/virtual interface that is established in relation to other group members. Among these, Spanish youth is, unquestionably, one of the most important social engines propelling ICT use in our country. Academics and journalists have creatively baptized this new generation with names such as *Cultura Messenger* (Gordo López, 2006), *Generation Tuenti* and *Generation 2.0.*[1] For this social group, which encompasses youngsters aged 12-20, Web 2.0. tools have become the most valued sources of information and vehicles for expression and participation (52%), followed by educational centers (40%), the press (29%), and cell phones (27,4%) (Gordo López, 2006: 46)[2]. Generation 2.0. members generally feel that Web 2.0. tools provide instant connectivity to a more authentic world that is shaped by its users (rather than media moguls) and generally connect to the web several times a week/day (Gordo López, 2006: 75).

Moreover, a more recent report carried out by the Universidad Camilo José Cela (2010), "Generación 2.0. 2010. Hábitos de los adolescentes en el uso de

---

1 *Generación Tuenti* is a buzzword currently used by several Spanish newspapers after the popular Spanish social network Tuenti, the younger sibling of Facebook – a national network mostly frequented by teenagers. Robin Mason and Frank Rennie refer to these youngsters as *Millenials* (following Oblinger & Oblinger, 2005), that is, those teenagers born since 1982 whose main behavioral characteristics are multitasking; image, sound and video preference over other textual platforms; networked interactions rather than "independent individual study"; and technological expertise (2008: 24-25). In this article we will mostly use the commonly understood label, *Generation 2.0.*, to refer to technologically active youth in Spain.

2 Gordo López *et. al.* base their conclusions on a national study carried out by Megías, E. entitled *Jóvenes y política. El compromiso de lo colectivo* (2005). Madrid: INJUVE/FAD, pages 78 and 360. Web 2.0. tools discussed by these authors include web pages, e-mail, chat, FTPs, blogs and discussion forums. They do not address the emergence of social networks, which grew in popularity in Spain approximately a year later. It is interesting to point out that, in this study, men valued the Internet higher than women, who still rate educational centers higher (43%) than men (33%). Furthermore, younger teenagers who were around 15-16 in 2005 showed an even higher preference for Web 2.0. applications than their older peers (Gordo López *et. al.*, 2006), and this is precisely the age group who has just entered tertiary education.

las redes sociales. Estudio comparativo entre comunidades autónomas", which selected 7,000 youngsters from different Spanish regions as subjects of study, concluded that 78% teenagers ages 12-17 habitually use social networks (80% Tuenti vs. 14% Facebook) (Universidad Camilo José Cela, UCJC, 2010) (see Figure 1).

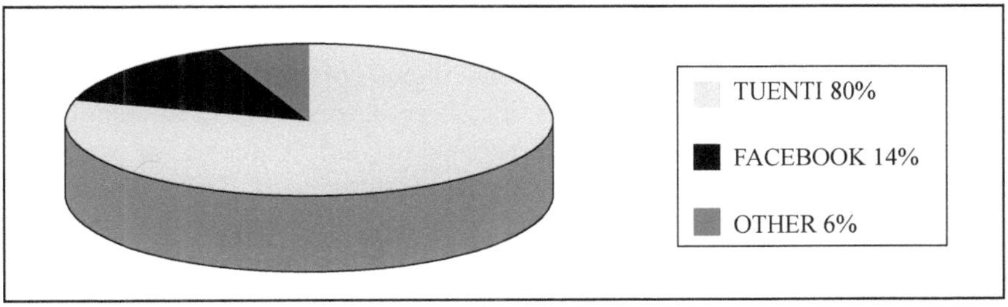

Fig. 1: Use of social networks by Spanish teenagers (based on UCJC, 2010)

Participants and methodology

Capitalizing on the popularity and potential of Web 2.0. tools, in October 2009, we introduced NING, a well-known educational social network site (ESNS), into our subject *English Language III* (Advanced English), an English Philology yearly module at the University of Valencia, Spain. This core module was team-taught by the two authors of this study for 10 months. It targeted 45 students, 35 of whom became active NING users with an average of 8-10 online contributions per month.[3] For an evening group whose ages ranged from 21 to 38, our subjects were not prototypical *Generation 2.0.* students. In fact, 42% admitted to rarely using social network sites (SNS). Hence, our network became, for many of them, an introduction to key digital literacies they will need to be familiar with in their future careers in the field of education. They themselves baptized

3 We would like to express our deepest gratitude to our colleagues at the UV Rosana Dolón and Helenia López, who taught the morning sections of this same subject, for their inspiration in the implementation of NING for classroom use. We would also like to thank all of our English Language III students for the numerous ideas and suggestions shared with us during the 2009/10 academic year. Needless to say, any faults in this study are purely our own. Additionally, we would like to stress the importance of establishing a generous and effective coordination between *teaching teams* and students in the EHEA – a practical matter that is not often sufficiently addressed in our degrees (Pérez Cañado, 2009).

our ESNS "*E3B: What's HappeNING?*" after a democratic online poll that registered many creative suggestions.[4]

Our main aims implementing an ESNS in the ESL classroom were to: 1. expand content learning and exposure to the foreign language introducing a friendly format we believed most students use on a daily basis; 2. foster participation by building an affective atmosphere that would motivate them while increasing engaged collective informal learning; 3. develop crucial competences in English Studies such as communicative and digital competences, as well as collaborative and autonomous learning skills; 4. go beyond traditional hierarchical classroom relations to create a multidirectional network of interactive peers that included the lecturers; 5. enable students to transfer their ICT skills, which are mostly focused on recreational communication activities, and facilitate their use for critical and educational self-improvement (e.g. learning to filter Web 2.0. contents in a critical manner). Last, we were aware of the fact that students have varying levels of ICT expertise and hoped to help them transfer that digital knowledge also among peers.

Data for this study was collected using the following qualitative instruments of analysis: 1. linguistic and audio-visual student output from the network itself; 2. two anonymous questionnaires completed by the students and aimed at monitoring their progress and real network usage; 3. biweekly conversations and reflective analysis carried out by the two lecturers/authors; 4. oral output given by students in class and 5. student academic results (i.e. specific assignments and exams that measured their linguistic improvement).

Educational social network sites: A definition

Although many interesting studies have surfaced in recent years analyzing the explosion of social networks and their various uses in higher education (Carrington & Robinson, 2009; Mason & Rennie, 2008), we have not found a description of *educational* social network sites that fits our premise: i.e. a network which takes into account both online and face-to-face classroom interactions. We consider educational social network sites (ESNSs) as communities of learners who habitually interact through multimodal online platforms but who may also meet in face-to-face settings in order to build a collaborative space that fosters en-

4 Our classroom gender distribution was typical of an English Philology group at the University of Valencia (68% women vs. 32% men). It is also interesting to point out that there was a high intercultural component in the network, as 16% of the students were Erasmus exchange students from other European countries such as France, Poland, Germany and Sweden. E3B stands for English Language Three, group B.

gaged participation, information-exchange and peer-advice as reflective and self-managed learning practices.

Our implementation of an educational social network site, NING, in *English Language III* thus addressed a key methodological change that has been favored in most EHEA academic discussions: the creation of a non-hierarchical and multidirectional setting that presents a team of teachers and students as interactive peers (Brígido Corachán, 2009; Pérez Cañado, 2009) – a setting which also provides a "flexible architecture" (Papacharissi, 2009) that fosters autonomous (non-teacher mediated) student exchanges leading to both formal and informal learning. Through a variety of applications that allow students to contact each other publically or privately in a bilateral or multidirectional manner, ESNSs entail a radical reconfiguration of the social space of the ESL classroom, helping students to take the lead in the communicative act.[5]

Educational social network sites in the ESL classroom, with their multiple, student-managed applications (forums, blogs, images, grammar activities, videos, comment wall, private inbox, etc.), which will be described in the following section, adopt somewhat a *rhizome* structure, a model for socio-political critique popularized by Deleuze & Guattari (1987) in their groundbreaking work *A Thousand Plateaus*. The *Oxford English Dictionary*, describes the rhizome as a "continuously growing, usually horizontal, underground stem which puts lateral shoots and adventitious roots at intervals" (online). We are seduced by this image of multiple and fluid roots with unexpected connections that are naturally de-centered, and would like to superimpose it over the traditional image of the vertical, hierarchical and teacher-centered tree of knowledge. Thus, we believe that ESNSs in the ESL classroom do not only enhance effective communication among peers in a foreign language, but also have the potential to be liberating, inspiring and motivating at the same time. Through multimodal, de-centered and collaborative interactions, ESNSs humbly follow Paulo Freire's (1996) recommendations for an effective critical pedagogy – helping to empower the traditionally shy or silenced student's voice in his/her construction of knowledge and in his/her critical understanding of the world. Furthermore, our ultimate objective was to build a collaborative network of peers that would continue to interact and assist one another after graduation.

5 It is important to remark that the ESNS of our choice, NING, enabled us to create private profiles within a restricted system that protected our students' data-exchanges and identities at all times.

Educational social network sites and competence building

One of the advantages brought about by introducing an ESNS in the context of our English language course was developing competences. In this blended-learning scenario – i.e., combining traditional face-to face tuition with online teaching (Heinze & Procter, 2004; Zaragoza Ninet & Clavel Arroitia, 2010), NING has indeed proved beneficial in order to build up students' communicative competence, of particular relevance in the context of foreign language teaching, especially if we consider the latest trends in the field. When Hymes (1972) described the term Communicative Competence, he purposefully linked grammar correction and social appropriateness. His definition embodies the main purpose of our educational social network: to help students strengthen their linguistic competence whilst developing further social skills. Communicative Competence primarily involves grammatical competence. This means that in order to communicate effectively, we need to promote a meaningful use of language (Savignon, 1983). In our classroom network, *E3B: What's HappeNING?,* grammatical competence has been developed through a balanced practice of three skills: listening, writing and reading.[6]

Let us describe the educational use of these applications in detail. Two sections in NING were specifically aimed at developing students' listening skills: a music section, where a wide range of audio material (mainly songs) were uploaded by both students and teachers, and a video section where users uploaded video material connected to what was being dealt with in class. In this way, we ensured the audio and video material also expanded content-learning such as new vocabulary, expressions and idioms.

Writing skills were targeted by means of the forum and blog sections, both of which were used as asynchronous discussion boards. Whereas the Forum was more free-form and had a rather social purpose such as the exchange of information (including casual debates around specific topics related to class content), more formal, instructive and reflective discussions were kept for the Blog space.

6 The development of oral skills was tackled by means of another class project: the creation of digital stories, which will be briefly discussed later in this chapter. For more information on this project, see Zaragoza Ninet & Brígido Corachán (2011).

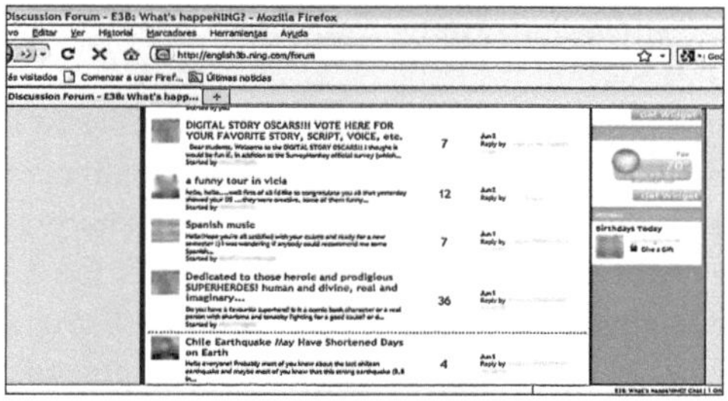

Fig. 2: *Forum Topics*

In *E3B: What's HappeNING?,* we also launched a synchronous discussion board - the chat section-, hoping to enhance the practice of pragmatic elements in the negotiation of meaning in a foreign language, as the chat is a medium that imitates the patterns of oral interaction (Pellettieri, in Warschauer & Kern, 2000). Though used, our chat was not a section that was particularly explored, maybe due to the fact that it was our first experience with multimodal educational social networks, and it was difficult to coordinate live sessions with such a great number of students. Delving into this particular application, studying how we can make it work efficiently to supplement class participation in a more spontaneous manner is one of our short-term commitments. This could be done by establishing *chat days* where, periodically, selected groups of students would talk online with the teachers about a chosen topic.[7]

With regards to reading skills, a section was created to upload articles directly related to class content. This section was, however, soon replaced by the blog itself, because the latter allowed student comments and was, thus, more interactive. For both of them, we selected engaging material to encourage reading and to elicit student feedback.

In addition to these articles (uploaded by teachers primarily), student comments in the discussion boards and comment walls in their personal profiles functioned simultaneously as input (writing skill), as well as communicative output (reading skill), for their peers, whose reactions (commentaries/suggestions/links for further reading) acted, in turn, as output for others and so on, exponentially expanding the learning cycle.

Finally, we devoted a specific section to the regular uploading of links to self-corrective online exercises so that students could more easily practice the new grammar items developed in every class unit. In this way, we tried to guar-

7 Successful projects using synchronous discussion boards (chat rooms) in the foreign language classroom to expand communicative competence and its assessment are, for example, Pellettieri (in Warschauer & Kern, 2000) and Oskoz (2005).

antee the expansion and acquisition of content learning, the first of our aims when introducing an ESNS in the subject. However, data show that only 38% of the students actually made use of this section, which may be due to the fact that they looked at the social network with a more recreational perspective.

NING has helped us tackle pragmatic skills too. The pragmatic component is a key factor in the Council of Europe report for the Common European Framework of Reference for Languages. According to Savignon, "the inadequacy of a four skills model of language use is now recognized", hence "the communicative competence needed for participation includes not only grammatical competence, but pragmatic competence" (1991: 282). Due to its rather social nature, the forum has proved a useful tool to put into practice a wide range of performative speech acts (Austin, 1962) such as giving information, offering, suggesting, advising, acknowledging or requesting. Student personal pages also exhibited extremely productive social exchanges, such as commenting positively on their peers' work, asking for advice, or apologizing.

Acquiring digital competence in the new EHEA degrees

Overall, we found the concept of digital competence particularly relevant to the new EHEA context, which fosters technological innovation. As we highlighted in the Participants and Methodology section above, by introducing an ESNS into an ESL classroom, our intention was to strengthen linguistic skills, while integrating and developing ICT proficiencies.

Firstly, we would like to emphasize two interrelated terms that are key in this respect: Digital Literacy, defined as "the ability to access digital media and ICT, to understand and critically evaluate different aspects of digital media and media contents and to communicate effectively in a variety of contexts" (Ala-Mutka, Punie & Redecker, 2008: 4), and Digital Competence, which refers to "the confident and critical use of ICT for employment, learning, self-development and participation in society" (Ala-Mutka, Punie & Redecker 2008: 3). We believe that acquiring Digital Competence under the EHEA is a fundamental project or mission for teachers and students. Thus, we all regularly assisted one another in our strife towards Digital Competence, mainly through the use of the educational social network and all its related ICT material (Forum/Youtube videos/Hyperlinking/Internet/Cultural photos/Chat). Additionally, we regularly made use of other applications from the Universitat de València's e-learning platform (Aula Virtual) – particularly its Task uploading section, where students submitted structured digital assignments, and its messaging board system, which was used to communicate with the whole group. To complement these efforts, our students embarked in the production of Digital Stories with specific video and audio software, as we will discuss further below.

Digital Storytelling (DS), the educational benefits of which have been largely explored by Bernard Robin (2006) and Carmen Gregori-Signes (2008), acts as

> a good way to engage students in both traditional and innovative ways of telling a story, since students learn how to combine some basic multimedia tools (e.g., graphics or animations) with activities as varied as doing research, writing, delivering presentations, using technology, interviewing, improving interpersonal skills, learning problem-solving techniques, and assessment expertise (Gregori-Signes, 2008: 43).

As we have discussed in an earlier work, these digital storytelling projects substituted the classical oral examination (Zaragoza Ninet & Brígido Corachán, 2011). Students exhibited and orally defended their digital stories on two programmed DS festivals, and these videos were later uploaded to the online social network platform so that every class member could vote for their favorite narratives and assess their peers' work.

Digital literacy requires constant training and updating. As members of the project ANGLOTIC, an innovative group of researchers in the Department of English and German Philology at the University of Valencia,[8] our onus is on creating and sharing digital material, exchanging new tools and information and, overall, keeping up with the latest trends in ICT implementation in our teaching methodologies. Teacher coordination and collaboration are essential in this context too:

> One of the major lessons we have learnt is that the introduction of ICTs cannot be carried out efficiently on an individual basis. Coordination and teamwork are at the heart of the move to less teacher-centred classes in which ICTs play a significant role (Pennock-Speck, 2013: 112).

Results: Toward self-managed, collaborative learning practices

Online educational social network sites enable students to adopt a type of interaction that is liberating and that strengthens autonomy in a more effective manner than traditional lecturing classroom practices, where teacher mediation and control are tighter. Through our ESNS hosted by NING, our students had

8 Anglotic is composed of lecturers from the Department of English and German Philology at the University of Valencia, all of whom are interested in blended-learning and in the creation of teaching/learning objects to foster the acquisition of competences in the EHEA context. For background information on the project and current activities, see the Anglotic website: http://www.uv.es/anglotic/.

the possibility to present themselves in a wider variety of visual and verbal styles and, although they often had to navigate what Thomas (2002) denominates "incoherent learning structures" in the discussion boards, they unquestionably developed a stronger sense of self-managed learning. Furthermore, they gained a higher degree of responsibility toward their learning progress and that of their peers, as the following student interaction, where Student A organizes and encourages peers to contribute to a discussion thread on book reviews, illustrates:

Thread started by Student A: What's the last book you've read?

First Posting by Student A:

Hi everybody! I thought one thing [...] we are talking about films, heroes, and a lot of things, but what book *are you* reading now? or *which one would you recommend me and our colleagues*? and please! I don't want to see "Beowulf" or things like that (I loved it, but it's now my past) *I'd like to know about your favourite books, what you read in your free time*. Now I'm reading "The Lovely Bones", in Spanish [...] but I have to read some books in Spanish because I share them with my mother and she doesn't know English! I'll comment you the book soon, now I'm starting it, but seems nice. The saga of "Twilight" is interesting, *addictive*, but it'll never be literature (in my opinion). Well, I'm a really *book-worm*, give me books to read!!! *(E3B What's Happening?* February 10th 2010, *our emphasis*)

In this first opening posting, Student A encourages her classmates to recommend books they have truly enjoyed reading and which differ from those canonical texts studied in class (*Beowulf*). She also introduces vocabulary studied in one of our ESL lessons on readers that very same month (*addictive, book-worm*). Her peers immediately start contributing suggestions and thank her for her idea: creating a platform of informal literary exchange that departs from institutionalized knowledge.

Student B: Nice topic, A!

Student C: Hi !!!I like the idea of talking about literature, (or "not literature", as A. would said) Good idea!!!! :)

Twenty-five postings later, 18 of which were contributed by peers and seven by Student A, as she regularly commented on her peers' choices, Student A thanks them collectively for their engaging suggestions and for their help with the thread:

Posting by Student A (*E3B: What's HappeNING?* March 2nd 2010, *our emphasis*)

I think I heard about this book, it sounds great, I agree with you, sometimes we need to read or see how other people live and how fortunated we are (in spite of the crisis!). *I like the way all of you are helping me with this post, THANKS TO ALL OF YOU!!!!!*

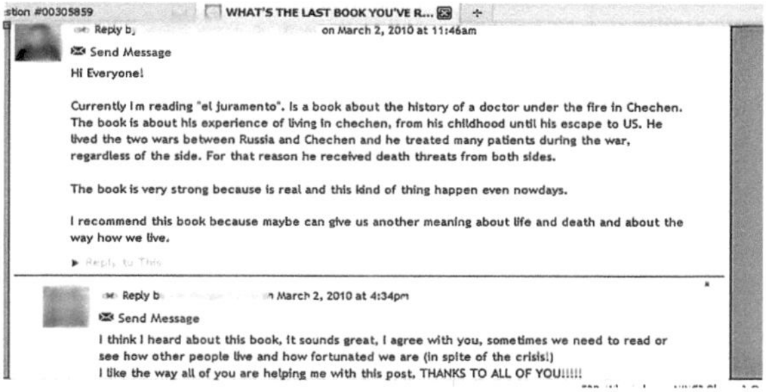

Fig. 3: *Student management of collective learning*

This particular forum thread ended up hosting 37 postings (only one of which was uploaded by an instructor) and spanned from early February until the beginning of June. It is interesting to point out that most of the book reviews contributed to the thread showed spontaneous and realistic language (including grammatical and lexical mistakes, as is expected in ESL learners) and presented more accurate portrayals of student knowledge, effort, and progress than the rather structured film reviews they had to hand in as part of the written portfolio of compositions that formally assessed their writing skills.[9] Students micro-managed this and many other threads entirely on their own – a practice which clearly strengthened confidence, team-work, and shared responsibility in their learning progress.

Furthermore, the network generated an unprecedented community of collaborators that went beyond the classroom level and which incorporated a lot of international Erasmus students. Observed collaborative practices in the online network included: 1. constant peer-guidance; 2. advice on professional outlets, job applications, and the spectrum of work possibilities after graduation; 3. planning of socio-cultural outings in Valencia such as classroom dinners and

9 We would like to remark that, at the beginning of the academic year, both instructors regularly corrected selected grammatical and lexical errors from the posts online so all students could benefit from correction. However, we soon realized that this practice inhibited many students' (ashamed of their linguistic abilities) participation. We decided then to proceed the rest of the year in a more flexible manner regarding their errors in the blogs, comment walls, and discussion boards (Thomas' incoherent learning structures), encouraging students instead to revise their information exchanges themselves and suggesting other tools for error correction such as tutorials during office hours, and online proofreading applications and dictionaries that would help them amend their own mistakes before posting. Although we believe that self-correction further strengthens a student's critical and responsible engagement with their learning practices, a higher emphasis should be laid on self-correcting before posting a message to the ESNS.

English-speaking tours of emblematic historical buildings around our city; 4. informal assessment of peer work.

Progressively, through the increased usage of our ESNS (with both its online and weekly face-to-face components), our community of learners was transformed into a social and professional community of peers that is, hopefully, still in contact and that provides professional assistance and emotional support after the academic year is over.[10]

Assessment of competences, autonomous and collaborative skills

Participation in our educational social network was assessed in terms of quality and not quantity, using a measuring scale adapted from Brígido Corachán (2009), which focused on the level of student cognitive engagement with the subject matter. ESNS participation accounted for 10% of the final grade – a percentage which also took into account student effort in his/her acquisition of communicative and digital competences, as well as other team-building skills such as the level and type of peer-to-peer interaction (taking the form of guidance, encouragement, appreciation, etc. and based on pragmatic cues as seen in Brígido Corachán, 2012). Instructors also took into account student information searching skills, content sharing, and critical reflection accompanying contributed material.

Digital stories (which further assessed student digital competence regarding some of the afore-mentioned ICT-management abilities) were evaluated separately by all instructors and students (20% of the final grade as discussed in Zaragoza Ninet & Brígido Corachán, 2011). These team-produced videos were also integrated into the ESNS as audiovisual input to further strengthen listening skills, and to obtain direct peer feedback.

Conclusions

Overall, students showed great satisfaction with NING: 85% highly recommended the use of online ESNSs in forthcoming years, and 81% of the students habitually using NING passed the subject with a good grade (B average) which, to us, was an excellent academic result when comparing it to previous years/levels.

---

10 This final part of the case study, following up on student contact and peer assistance after graduation, is still pending.

Even more rewarding was the certainty that our online educational social network site had enabled our students to adopt liberating interactions that fostered autonomy and encouraged responsible self-management of learning practices. Our students presented a wide variety of visual and verbal styles fitting their personalities, ages, and learning methodologies. Despite their variety of approaches and interactions, all students regularly searched, filtered and critically commented on shared materials for specific tasks they themselves launched and managed. Furthermore, the network fostered the creation of a community of collaborators that surpassed average classroom solidarity practices; thus, a group of learners was transformed into a social and professional community of peers.

Indeed, this project has also faced many shortcomings and there is considerable room for improvement. Although enthusiastic about the network at first, a great number of students soon expressed concern for their time limitations, as some could only participate in a sparse manner and only with considerable sacrifices of their social or available study time. Some (22%) simply could not participate at all. We thus recommend that time spent in ESNSs be incorporated and quantified as subject hours in the description of the module and be accounted for.

As we mentioned at the beginning of this chapter, with an average age higher than usual, our subjects were not a Generation 2.0. prototype. Some of them were not familiar with ICTs (42% actually admitted to rarely using online SNS) and, hence, bridging the wide divide between more technologically savvy students and less habitual ICT users was not always easy. Hence, more work to help students transfer digital skills among peers (including the instructors) will be needed in future implementations of the ESNS. Even though future generations will most likely be familiar with ICTs (Generation 2.0. is now in first/second year of our English Studies degree at the University of Valencia), we believe that a greater effort will be required to facilitate the transfer of Generation 2.0. digital capital from the social to the educational fields.

According to Mason & Rennie,

> Critics of user-created content refer to a breakdown in the traditional place of expertise, authority and scholarly input. They express concerns about trust, reliability and believability in relation to the move away from the printed word to the more ephemeral digital word. (2008: 6).

A conscious effort will also be needed to help students filter critically these vast amounts of online, user-generated information. This is actually one of the goals fostered by the EHEA: the development of critical thinking skills in a world we are constantly interacting with and which is no longer merely physical. Although these same critics believe that "new technologies encourage a short attention span and lead students to demand immediate answers, rather than thinking for themselves" (in Mason & Rennie, 2008: 7), this will always depend on the tasks we make them carry out using Web 2.0. applications, and on our effective monitoring of these. Teacher guidance and mediation are still crucial and, in large groups, we recommend that instructors have teaching assistants (or more advanced students) helping them oversee the discussion boards. Students should also be encouraged to attend teacher tutorials regularly and to use easily accessible error correction software (spell-checkers, grammar checking, or online dictionaries) in order to reinforce their autonomy in the acquisition of communicative competence.

A last issue we would like to raise is that digital technologies are often unreliable, in the sense that a free online platform may suddenly establish payment plans, or have technical problems that may go beyond the instructor's control. This happened to us with NING, which suddenly stopped their free service at the end of the academic year.[11] Keeping up-to-date with the most innovative, reliable and effective systems through peer interaction with colleagues and students will hopefully help us face these and other technological challenges.

Bibliography

Ala-Mutka, K., Puni, Y., & Redecker, C. (2008). *Digital Competence for Lifelong Learning*. Luxembourg: Office for Official Publications of the European Communities. Retrieved from http://ftp.jrc.es/EURdoc/JRC48708.TN.pdf (01/01/2013).

Austin, J. L. (1962). *How to Do Things With Words*. Oxford: Oxford University Press.

Bartlett-Bragg, A. (2006). Reflections on pedagogy: Reframing practice to foster informal learning with social software. Retrieved from http://digitaldialogues.blogs.com/learning_technologies/ (01/01/2013).

Brígido Corachán, A. M. (2009). From the virtual forum to the classroom: Developing cognitive engagement and critical thinking skills through online and face-to-face student discussions. *Lenguaje y Textos*, *229*, 141–153.

Brígido Corachán, A. M. (2012). A pragmatic study of peer-tutoring and peer-assessment practices in online literary forums. In *Teaching English as a Foreign Language: Proposals for the Language Classroom*. València: Perifèric.

Carrington, V., & Robinson, M. (2009). *Digital Literacies. Social Learning and Classroom Practices*. Los Angeles/London: UKLA-Sage.

---

11 Although NING has facilitated the sponsoring of educational social networks, with the help of Pearson, for example, this option is only available to networks based in the United States and it covers the basic plan only, from which some of the most popular NING applications are missing. Switching to another online provider offers, however, no guarantees that the site will stay free and, unfortunately, not all academic institutions are in a position to finance online ESNS service for their staff.

Deleuze, G., & Guattari, F. (1987). *A Thousand Plateaus. Capitalism and Schizophrenia*. London: University of Minnesota Press.

Freire, P. (1996). *Pedagogía del oprimido*. Madrid: Siglo XXI.

Gordo López, A. L. (Coord.). (2006). *Jóvenes y cultura messenger. Tecnología de la información y la comunicación en la sociedad interactiva*. Madrid: Injuve.

Gregori-Signes, C. (2008). Integrating the old and the new: Digital storytelling in the EFL language classroom. *GRETA Journal*, *16*(1–2), 43–50.

Heinze, A., & Procter, C. T. (2004). Reflections on the use of blended learning. In *Education in a Changing Environment*, 13-14 September 2004, University of Salford, UK. Retrieved from http://usir.salford.ac.uk/1658/ (01/01/2013).

Hymes, D. H. (1972). On communicative competence. In J. B. Pride & J. Holmes (Eds.), *Sociolinguistics. Selected Readings* (pp. 269–293). Harmondsworth: Penguin.

Mason, R., & Rennie, F. (2008). *E-Learning and Social Networking Handbook. Resources for Higher Education*. New York/London: Routledge.

Oblinger, D. G., & Oblinger, J. L. (2005). Is it age or IT: First steps toward understanding the Net Generation. In D. G. Oblinger & J. L. Oblinger (Eds.), *Educating the Net Generation* (pp. 2.1-2.20). Louisville/Washington: Educause. Retrieved from http://www.educause.edu/educatingthenetgen (01/01/2013).

Oskoz, A. (2005). Students' dynamic assessment via online chat. *CALICO Journal, 22*(3), 513–536.

Papacharissi, Z. (2009). The virtual geographies of social networks: A comparative analysis of Facebook, LinkedIn and ASmallWorld. *New Media and Society*, *11*(1–2), 199–220.

Pasadas Ureña, C. (2010). Multiliteracy and social networks in higher education. In *Information and Digital Competencies in Higher Education* (online monograph), *Revista de Universidad y Sociedad del Conocimiento (RUSC)*, *7*(2). Retrieved from http:rusc.uoc.edu/ojs/index.php/rusc/article/view/v7n2-pasadas/v7n2-pasadas-eng (01/01/2013).

Pérez Cañado, M. L. (2009). Debunking EHEA myths: Common ECTS misconceptions and why they are wrong. *International Education Studies*, *2*(4), 15–24.

Pennock, B. (2009). European convergence and the role of ICE in English studies at the Universitat de València. In M. L. Pérez Cañado (Ed.), *English Language Teaching in the European Credit Transfer System*: *Facing the Challenge* (pp. 169-185). Frankfurt am Main: Peter Lang.

Pennock-Speck, B. (2013). Teaching competences through ICTs in an English degree programme in a Spanish setting. In M. L. Pérez Cañado (Ed.), *Competency-based Language Teaching in Higher Education* (pp. 107–118). Amsterdam: Springer.

Robin, B. (2006). The educational uses of Digital Storytelling. University of Houston. Retrieved from digitalstorytelling.coe.uh.edu (01/01/2013).

Savignon, S. J. (1983). *Communicative Competence: Theory and Classroom Practice*. Reading, MA: Addison-Wesley.

Savignon, S. J. (1991). Communicative language teaching: State of the art. *TESOL Quarterly* *25*(2), 261–277.

Thomas, M. J. W. (2002). Learning within incoherent structures: The space of online discussion forums. *Journal of Computer Assisted Learning* *18*(3), 351–358.

Universidad Camilo Jose Cela (2010). *Informe: Generación 2.0. Hábitos de los adolescentes en el uso de las redes sociales. Estudio comparativo entre comunidades autónomas*. Retrieved from http://www.slideshare.net/ucjc/generacin-20-hbitos-de-los-ad (01/01/2013).

Warschauer, M., & Kern, R. (2000). *Network-based Language Teaching: Concepts and Practice.* Cambridge: Cambridge University Press.

Yus, F. (2010). Nuevas formas de interacción en Internet: Los sitios de redes sociales y los mundos virtuales tridimensionales. *II Jornadas sobre Lengua y Tecnología.* Universidad Politécnica de Valencia, May 2010 (oral communication).

Zaragoza Ninet, M. G., & Clavel Arroitia, B. (2010). La enseñanza del inglés a través de una metodología blended-learning: Cómo mejorar el método tradicional. *Lenguaje y Textos, 31*, 25–35.

Zaragoza Ninet, M. G., & Brígido Corachán, A. M. (2011). Creative evaluation of communicative competence through Digital Story. *The Grove: Working Papers on English Studies 18*, 285–307.

The Use of ICT for Competence Teaching: A Practical Approach at the University of Valencia

Sergio Maruenda-Bataller & Begoña Clavel-Arroitia

Abstract

Language learning theory and practice has evolved from a highly guided to a more open learning process. This is a consequence of the incorporation of previous degree structures into the European Higher Education Area (EHEA) consolidation process. In this chapter, we describe our experience in the use of blended-learning methodology and also look at some possible drawbacks its implementation may bring.

In the next few lines, we summarize the theoretical bases for our methodology and we offer a review of current literature on blended-learning. We also describe a series of Information and Communication Technology (ICT) tools and the way in which they have been used in different modules in the Degree of English Studies at the *Facultat de Filologia, Traducció i Comunicació* of the *Universitat de València*. Our objective is to point out the advantages and drawbacks of the implementation of the ICTs employed in our degree through the description of our own experience. We try to demonstrate how their implementation has acted as a powerful catalyst for higher achievement. After that, we give a brief overview of the topic of competence assessment and show an example of its adaptation in order to evaluate one of the ICT tools we describe. Finally, we offer some suggestions on the use of ICTs and map out some future directions for research.

Introduction

In this chapter, we describe our experience in the use of a blended-learning methodology as English Language lecturers and explain how the use of new technologies can improve the quality of the teaching and learning processes. In the next few lines, we outline the main theories on which we base our methodology and offer a review of current literature on blended-learning. We then explain a series of particular tools and the way in which they have been implemented in different modules in the Degree of English Studies at the Universitat de València in the framework of the *AngloTIC Project*.[1] We intend to show the advantages and drawbacks of the implementation of these particular ICT tools. We also provide a specific proposal for competence assessment using a standard definition of competence for ICT-formats.

---

1 *AngloTIC: Creation of teaching materials and learning objects for English language and linguistics* is a consolidated innovation group recognized and financed by the Educational Innovation Unit at the Universitat de València (http://www.uv.es/anglotic).

Theoretical principles

We base the implementation of our methodology on a series of theoretical principles that we describe in this section. We adopt Krashen's (1982) Monitor Model, which claims that there are two differentiated processes: acquisition and learning. Whereas learning is a conscious process through which we focus on several linguistic aspects and which usually takes place inside the classroom, the acquisition process occurs naturally when we receive messages that we can understand, which is what he calls comprehensible input. This key concept in his theory implies that comprehensible input is the only way in which language can be acquired. Our purpose is to give our students the opportunity to learn through a series of varied activities so that they are exposed to language extensively and will eventually acquire it (Zaragoza Ninet & Clavel Arroitia, 2008).

Gee (1992) suggests that we acquire a language subconsciously by exposure to a model, through a trial and error process, and practice within social groups, normally without formal teaching, and that is precisely what we want to promote through the methodology used at our university. We consider that meaningful learning is a vital concept, since it takes place when the student is able to select the most important information in a particular context, to organise it into a logical mental framework and to integrate the new information with existing information (Mayer, 1997).

Taking into consideration that the use of new technologies can improve the acquisition of meaningful knowledge, we can then assert that, according to Mayer's (1997) Generative Theory of Multimedia Instruction, when we apply mixed modes of delivery (texts, graphics, audio, video, animation, etc.), learners put cognitive processes to work in order to acquire knowledge. Thus, multimedia learning takes place when our students are able to construct mental representations through words and images presented to them in a text format containing illustrations, narrations and animations. Following this, Mayer (2003) explains that an educational multimedia message is a type of presentation that includes words and images and that has been designed to foster meaningful learning. He also affirms that students learn best when they have access to visual and verbal representations and they interact simultaneously in their memory. According to what he labels The Multimedia Effect, students can learn better from well-designed multimedia messages through which they can build mental representations from words and pictures than from more traditional modes of communication involving words alone. Sweller (1999) highlights that multimedia products used in the educational background can be beneficial only if they are carefully designed and do not unnecessarily overload human information processing.

The increasing use of new technologies in the classroom has brought about a new teaching approach that promotes a major change in the teaching-learning process. Starting from a traditionally product-based, teacher-centred perspective, we have evolved to a student-centred, process-oriented model (Clavel Arroitia & Zaragoza Ninet, 2010).

The implementation of this new learning model involves taking into account collaborative learning, which posits that students learn best when they are actively involved in an activity and that students working in small groups tend to learn more of what is taught and retain it longer than when the same content is presented in other instructional formats. In spite of the many advantages of ICTs in our teaching practice, Pennock Speck (2009) warns that we must always bear in mind that the use of new technologies should only replace traditional methods if they offer tangible advantages and that they should be avoided if they require too much effort on the part of teachers and students and/or are too expensive. Interaction among our students, or peer interaction, should then be promoted in the classroom setting. Toussaint Clark & Clark (2008) assert that group dynamics can act as catalyst to obtain better results in the final product of a particular task and in the interpersonal relation among students. In effect, teamwork is an important general competence in our degree (see Pennock Speck, 2013).

One final important aspect to be taken into account is the fact that our students must be treated as adults and, therefore, we have to make them aware that they are responsible for their own learning process. Knowles' (1975) Andragogy Theory attempts to develop a context that is specifically aimed at adult learning. This author emphasizes that adults are self-directed and are expected to take responsibility for the decisions they make. Therefore, we must consider that instruction for adults needs to focus less on the content being taught and more on the process. Activities centred on case studies, role-playing, simulations, and self-evaluation are probably the most useful (Morland & Bivens, 2004). In activities of this type, according to a constructivist conception of education, the instructor adopts the role of facilitator rather than lecturer or grader, the learner becomes a constructor of meaning and technology has an influence on both roles (Sánchez Sola, 2006). The use of activities of this type supports the problem-centred orientation required for successful adult learning and promotes task-oriented and self-directed types of strategies, which imply the application of the principles of Andragogy (Morland & Bivens, 2004).

All this leads us to adopt a blended-learning methodology. We can define it as "a combination of technology and classroom instruction in a flexible approach to learning that recognizes the benefits of delivering some training and assessment online but also uses other modes to make up a complete training program which can improve outcomes and/or save costs" (Bañados, 2006: 534).

It is generally assumed that "blended-learning has come to be understood as a combination of conventional classroom instruction and e-learning" and that "blended-learning processes are thus articulated by combining online learning and traditional learning approaches in various degrees" (Gregorio Godeo, 2005: 1). According to Sharma & Barrett (2007: 7), blended-learning is "a language course which combines a face-to-face classroom component with an appropriate use of technology". Contrary to e-learning approaches, this is a model enabling the teaching and learning of competencies.

Our objective when teaching different modules in the Degree in English Studies within a blended-learning framework is that students may reach three goals: (1) acquire curricular knowledge, (2) learn English and (3) master ICT. Through ICT integration in the teaching methodology, students acquire *competencies* other than merely cognitive ones, i.e. associated to the acquisition of curricular knowledge (Zaragoza Ninet & Clavel Arroitia, 2010).

ICTs in classroom university teaching

The use of corpora and concordance tools

Our use of corpora focuses on vocabulary acquisition in the framework of corpus linguistics. We analyse the type of productive vocabulary that post-intermediate and advanced students employ and explore how its acquisition could be enhanced by the lecturers' implementation of corpus linguistics and research in a classroom setting. As Seidlhofer (2002) has suggested, collecting a learner corpus containing the output of these students can be helpful in various ways, since it allows us to detect specific problems and thus becomes a powerful tool in the development of more effective vocabulary patterns within the academic context. Different teachers have successfully applied this tool in different modules in our degree, but here we will only refer to its implementation in a particular subject: English Grammar.

Today several corpora are freely accessible through the Internet (for instance, the *Collins Cobuild Concordancer*, or the *British National Corpus*) and they can be exploited in numerous ways. We also consider that the analysis of specialised corpora, or sub-corpora, where attention can be focused on particular fields or registers, produces invaluable insights into native and non-native usage in specific discourse areas. Further, the collection of a learner corpus helps to identify common areas of difficulty for a particular group of students. Finally, the selective use of native and non-native corpora with programmes such as *AntConc* or *Wordsmith* can become extremely helpful in informing classroom practice and materials design (Fuster Márquez & Clavel Arroitia, 2010). We have attempted to determine the acceptance of corpus in the English classroom by students. We planned two sessions with a selected group of fourth-year students. We first prepared a workshop and presented them with a series of activities based on conclusive discourse markers and their collocations (see Figure 1.1).

We also introduced the use of the *Collins Cobuild Concordance Sampler* and carried out a number of searches. At the end of the workshop, we asked them to write an essay and then analysed their production. We then had another session in which we showed them some of the uses of conclusive discourse markers in their own production. They could observe the abuse of certain formulas and the incorrect use of some expressions (see Figure 1).

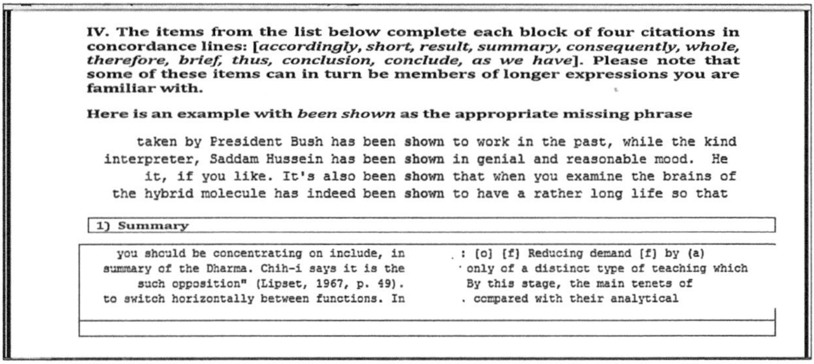

IV. The items from the list below complete each block of four citations in concordance lines: [*accordingly, short, result, summary, consequently, whole, therefore, brief, thus, conclusion, conclude, as we have*]. Please note that some of these items can in turn be members of longer expressions you are familiar with.

Here is an example with *been shown* as the appropriate missing phrase

taken by President Bush has been shown to work in the past, while the kind
interpreter, Saddam Hussein has been shown in genial and reasonable mood. He
it, if you like. It's also been shown that when you examine the brains of
the hybrid molecule has indeed been shown to have a rather long life so that

1) Summary

you should be concentrating on include, in . : [o] [f] Reducing demand [f] by (a)
summary of the Dharma. Chih-i says it is the · only of a distinct type of teaching which
such opposition" (Lipset, 1967, p. 49). By this stage, the main tenets of
to switch horizontally between functions. In . compared with their analytical

Fig. 1: Activity designed following Data Driven Learning (DDL)

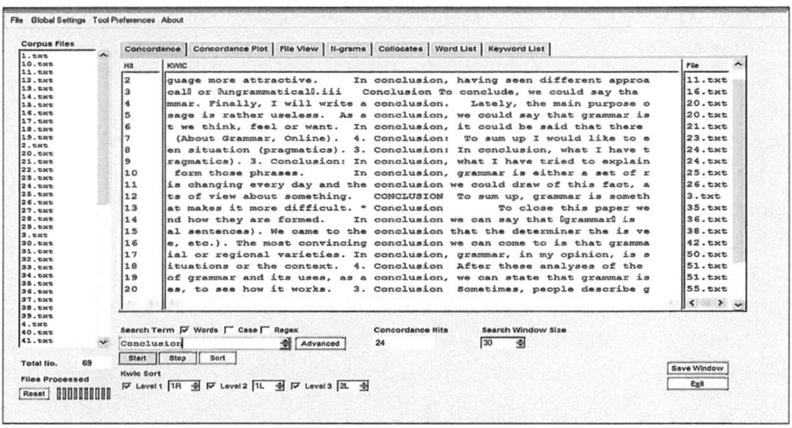

Fig. 2: Screen showing the use of a conclusive discourse marker by students

It was quite an interactive type of activity and students actively participated in the detection of mistakes. We must state that the use of corpora in this module is only sporadic and our intention was to test its potential in an actual classroom situation. Our students answered a questionnaire at the end of the second workshop and the results were very positive, as they showed their unanimous acceptance. We can conclude that the use of different corpora can be interesting and appropriate inside and outside the classroom and by both teachers and students.

Digital presentations: Digital Storytelling and Cuadernia

According to Gregori Signes (2008), a series of authors (Barrett, 2004, 2006a, 2006b; Robin, 2005, 2007, 2008) argue that Digital Storytelling (DS) is a good way to engage students in both traditional and innovative ways of telling a story, as students learn how to combine some basic multimedia tools with activities as varied as doing research, writing, delivering presentations, using technology, interviewing, improving interpersonal skills, learning problem-solving techniques, and applying assessment expertise.

The Bologna Process is promoting innovation in teaching with great emphasis on technology. Technology is forcing teachers and researchers to rethink the curriculum in most academic disciplines in terms of content and teaching and DS is a genre that seems to fit these demands, for it is a flexible and adaptable tool that may suit diverse purposes. Its main advantage is that it promotes the inclusion of the student's point of view and helps develop a series of skills which are essential for the students in our degree (research and writing skills, organization skills, technology skills, presentation skills, interpersonal skills, or problem-solving skills, which, in turn, develop digital literacy, global literacy, technology literacy, visual literacy, or information literacy). We have used this specific tool in EFL contexts such as English Language I, II and III, but also in other modules more related to literature, as is the case of Stylistics, where students produced digital versions of detective stories (cf. Alcantud Díaz, 2008).

Cuadernia is a similar tool that has been successfully used in English Language and Grammar groups. It is a tool which the Education and Science Department of the Region of Castilla la Mancha has made available for the educational community in order to create and promote the use of digital educational materials. It is also a free software tool and has been implemented in primary and secondary schools before its introduction in the context of higher degree studies. It offers some interesting possibilities, such as the incorporation of multimedia material as an active part of the student's project. *Cuadernia* promotes the creativity of students and enhances their oral presentations in different subjects.

Podcasting and videocasting

Research on pragmatics has demonstrated the relevance of inferential mechanisms on the interpretation of meaning and the importance of interpreters' activated schemata. The implications of these assumptions for the teaching of listening and speaking skills show that videocasts, with the strong support of the image dimension, allow learners to apply their interpretive skills more effectively than in traditional audio-recordings. Teaching using the latter is based on a linear approach, where training is often presented in a disconnected and decontextualized way and assessment is merely summative. The outcome of this approach is learner deficit in discourse management and *active* listening, reading, meaning production and writing.

Bou Franch & Maruenda (2009) describe the implementation of podcasting and videocasting in the practice modules of *English Language II (C1)* at the University of Valencia, together with the exploitation of methodological strategies, such as for instance the exploitation of blogs. In this way, the effective use of ICT and active teaching methods foster not only linguistic, but also social and collaborative competencies. The starting point is that aural-oral comprehension and production are complex cognitive and social communicative processes that are situated in discourse.

In the design of audiovisual tasks, these needs will be accounted for in the following steps[2]:

- *Pre-viewing activities*: they include the presentation of the objectives and the linguistic information in context. Tasks help activate socio-cultural schemata in order to anticipate meaning.
- *Viewing*: Audiovisual linguistic input is contextualised.
- *Post-viewing:* in order to reinforce new knowledge. It can be linked to other FL activities such as oral or written production.

Subtitling

Present-day market demands on translators, in terms of competencies and specialisation, have notably influenced their professional reality. From this perspective, translator training programmes (largely based on the old *read-and-translate*

2 For a sample activity and tutorial, visit: http://www.uv.es/anglotic/maruenda/Subtitling/.

approach) must implement, in addition to proficient language command in the working languages, cross-disciplinary knowledge and skills such as documentation, terminology, correcting/editing, and, of course, knowledge and management of ICT tools (Aula.int, 2005). Therefore, a shift from "teacher-centred" to "learning-centred classrooms" is also needed in translation (Kiraly, 1999).

Our research within translation focuses on the configuration of a model for assessment with specific competence-acquiring indicators, similar to those used for English language subjects (see *Competence assessment* below). This work combines methodological and practical approaches in the classroom. On the one hand, technical discussions of translation-theoretical notions are instantly and directly linked to practical issues in translation. On the other hand, students work on simulated translation projects involving their adoption of *professional* roles (project manager, translator, documenter, terminologist, and corrector/editor), where they learn to use ICT tools for creating translation memories, databases, subtitling, selecting documents, and publishing their materials online. Translation projects consist in translation commissions with strictly defined principles in terms of clients, target audiences, text function, etc., designed to test attainment of the competencies, which mirror the contents developed in the classroom.

In this context, our teaching of subtitling tools is part of the third-year obligatory subject *Translation from and into English of non-specialised texts* in English Studies. Specifically, our activities focus on the practice and subsequent evaluation of synthetic translation strategies, synchronising and summarising competence. We take advantage of the fact that subtitling software is freely accessible on the Internet: *Subtitle Workshop 4* (http://subtitle-workshop.softonic.com). After a hands-on workshop where learners are presented with the tool and a professional environment is simulated, they are asked to work on a translation commission dealing with subtitling a TV advertisement.

Competence assessment

In current theories, both competence assessment and individual guidance are conceived as cross-curricular processes that have a role throughout the teaching-learning stages; that is, as formative and reflective components accompanying the construction of students' learning. In this approach, since the planning of activities involves some individual and shared knowledge-building and heterogeneity of learning styles, it becomes essential to devise various methods for competence assessment or to implement those that best accommodate the students' curriculum and learning styles.

A competence model based on process therefore involves active participation through learning rather than passive reception of teaching. It cannot be conceived as improvised or isolated from syllabus design and teaching development. The latter is commonplace in summative assessment, which is oriented to attest the degree of attainment, while being limited to supporting the teacher's decision on the (non-) promotion of students. In this context, (1) learners play no role in setting goals or assessment criteria (they only undergo tests) and (2) knowledge about the criteria, required levels, tasks or questions must be inferred informally during training or in the often-scarce instructions in the course syllabus.

While correctly acknowledging what competencies imply, we are often misguided in the methodology associated with their instruction. If not explicitly addressed or included in Higher Education teaching, we are certainly putting their coverage on the line. As Pérez Cañado (2009: 1) states, "regrettably [...] critical thinking skills, creativity, problem solving, or capacity to adapt to new situations are precisely the ones [...] to be least developed and evaluated in Higher Education language degrees".

Systematic assessment must therefore be a guiding tool through the teaching-learning process that implies that design of the means and specific stages to be used to give students the necessary information: decision on the evaluation system (assessment situations), instruments (assignments), resources and strategies for evidence collections (as shown in the tables below). Evaluation must be a coherently planned method, interwoven in teaching unfolding. It cannot be conceived as a disjoint subject in the planning phases.

The objective is then to conceive the means for an actual formative evaluation. And in order to measure reliably someone's ability to do something, there must be clearly defined and widely accessible standards through which performance is measured and accredited (Smith, 2005). Figure 3 shows the indicators for the assessment an ICT competence, and can be adjusted to meet the requirements of a particular task or a particular subject. Thus, ICTs are both a means in itself and an instrument for measuring performance and competence degree of attainment, and become an integral part of the planning stage. This is the rationale behind the conducted methodology in our language and translation subjects.

INDICATORS	Competence Assessment Standard *Communicate effectively in visual, oral, written and ICT-formats, showing clear awareness of audience and purpose, for example, in role play scenarios, presentations and other tasks.*			
	Test PIE (instructor)	Objective criteria (instructor)	Interview / tutorial (instructor)	Questionnaire / co-evaluation (students)
	Writing assignment Aural comprehension: videocast	Competencies checklist	Oral comprehension and production Portfolio: individual and group work	Questionnaire / Portfolio on group work
Planning and organisation of debate				
Data collection		During the activity		
Planning and organisation of oral presentation				
Data collection		During the activity	Before the activity	During the activity
Selective search and management of information and resources				
Data collection		During and after work	Before the activity	
Knowledge of content: linguistic and discursive aspects (individual)				
Data collection	Follow schedule: after the activity		After the activity	After the activity
Knowledge of content: thematic aspects (individual)				
Data collection	Follow schedule: after the activity		After the activity	After the activity
Formative evaluation (%)	35	20	35	10
Summative evaluation (%)	40		40	20

Fig. 3: Standard indicators for competence assessment

Indicators	Criteria for the assessment of the competence: *Communicate effectively in visual, oral, written and ICT-formats, showing clear awareness of audience and purpose, for example, in role play scenarios, digital presentations and other tasks.*			
	Fully competent (88-100%)(9-10)	Competent (76-87%)(7-8,9)	Acceptable (60-75%)(5-6,9)	Not yet competent (<60%)(<5)
Planning and organisation of the digital / oral presentation	Applies organisation and sound argumentation criteria effectively. Applies discursive strategies (list of three, rhetorical questions, modality, contrast, figurative language, etc.) effectively to give clarity to their contribution.	Works out competently the mapping of structures on functional categories. Applies *some* discursive strategies (list of three, rhetorical questions, modality, contrast, figurative language, etc.) effectively to give clarity to their contribution.	Knows the structures of organisation of discourse and argumentation, but applies less than 50% or with errors. Knows discursive strategies (list of three, rhetorical questions, modality, contrast, figurative language, etc.), but not applied effectively to give clarity.	Doesn't know the structures of organisation of discourse and argumentation required at this level. Doesn't know discursive strategies at the required level, nor applies them.
Grammar and language usage	Use of elevated, persuasive and precise language. Use of *advanced* linguistic-discursive resources (vocabulary, structure, fluency, pronunciation). Contribute to clarity, style and language development.	Use of *advanced* linguistic-discursive resources (vocabulary, structure, fluency, pronunciation), though lacking precision and richness. Errors did not detract from the story.	Limited use of linguistic-discursive resources (vocabulary, structure, fluency, pronunciation). Grammar and usage are typically correct but errors detract from the story.	Deficient use of linguistic-discursive resources (vocabulary, structure, fluency, pronunciation). Repeated errors in grammar and usage distracted greatly from the story.
Knowledge of content, selective search and use of information and resources.	Selection of information is adequate for the purpose of the activity and the audience. Very good critical analysis of socio-cultural aspects related to the topic of the activity. Effective use of ICT to enrich presentation. Originality. Technological competence.	Selection of information is adequate for the purpose of the activity and the audience. Correct analysis of socio-cultural aspects related to the topic of the activity. ICT effectively contributes to adding meaning to the activity.	Part of the selected information is not adequate for the purpose of the activity and the audience. Superficial analysis of socio-cultural aspects related to the topic of the activity. Uses ICT sufficiently. Needs originality and resources.	The selected information is neither adequate nor sufficient for the purpose of the activity. There is no critical reflection on socio-cultural aspects related to the topic of the activity. Insufficient knowledge of ICT tools to achieve the goals.

Fig. 4: Standard definition of competence for ICT-formats: Digital Storytelling and Cuadernia

It is essential to provide students with the relevant information to progress during the whole process, by means of either individual tutorials or formal indicators. This can be done through:

- Previous specification of a reference or standard of performance to determine assessment criteria (see Figure 4).
- Systematization of evidence collection: identification of assessment situations and assignments.
- Decisions with regard to the evaluation system, instruments, resources and strategies for evidence collection.

Conclusions

Transforming the teaching-learning process into a shared, constructive and *visible* experience is one of the main priorities of the research group AngloTIC, which is working on the implementation of blended-learning and material design through ICT at the University of Valencia. From this perspective, our task as regards teaching methods is to plan and design a series of learning objectives which implement activities oriented towards developing discipline-specific content and competencies that are coherent with the expected learning outcomes and with efficient monitoring. With this in mind, this chapter has focused on adumbrating a small part of the work currently being done by AngloTIC.

One of the foundations of the project, therefore, is to make learners take on the role of *co-constructors* of knowledge and to be in touch with social and working environments through the elaboration of projects, problem-solving activities and use of professional tools. In this way, the fundamental reason for the incorporation of ICT is to stimulate the acquisition and development of competencies and it has become essential in every stage of the learning/acquisition process. In their new roles as facilitators, teachers will deploy effective strategies and design the materials that ease the attainment of the learning goals, also taking on board in the selection such factors as cognitive maturity, size and heterogeneity, subject, time, degree of autonomy, ability to motivate, etc.

For five years now, the English and German Department at the University of Valencia has been piloting an Innovation in Education Project as an initiative to meet the educational and methodological challenges in EHEA prior to the implementation of the new degree in English Studies in the academic year 2010/11. Together with the ICT tools illustrated in this article, the issue of competence assessment is one of our main concerns and, we deem, one of our major undertakings in the years to come. We concur with Pérez Cañado (2009: 2) that "we are still sorely lacking in empirically validated proposals for the implementation and assessment of competencies, an area which is in urgent need of research and will undoubtedly open new avenues for future investigations". Her research project at the University of Jaén is a constant source of inspiration and ideas for us. The model we have presented here is an inceptive yet attested proposal with specific indicators for competence description and clearly defined stages for data gathering which may be adapted to other competencies. It is designed to contribute modestly to the ongoing debate and is high on the agenda of the AngloTIC group for the immediate future.

Bibliography

Alcantud Díaz, M. (2008). Innovation, motivation and sustainable development in second cycle of English. *Proceedings of INTED 2008* [CD-ROM]. Valencia: IATED.

Aula.int. (2005). Translator training and modern market demands. *Perspectives: Studies in Translatology, 13*(2), 132–142.

Bañados, E. (2006). A blended-learning pedagogical model for teaching and learning EFL successfully through an online interactive multimedia environment. *CALICO Journal, 23*(3), 533–550.

Barrett, H. C. (2004). Tutorials for Digital Storytelling. Retrieved from http://electronicportfolios.org/digistory/ (01/01/13).

Barrett, H. C. (2006a). Researching and evaluating Digital Storytelling as a deep learning tool. *Proceedings of the 2006 Society for Information Technology and Teacher Education Conference*. Retrieved from http://electronicportfolios.org/portfolios/SITEStorytelling2006.pdf (01/01/13).

Barrett, H. C. (2006b). Digital Stories in ePortfolios: Multiple purposes and tools. Retrieved from http://electronicportfolios.org/digistory/purposesmac.html (01/01/13).

Bou Franch, P., & Maruenda, S. (2009). Pragmatica intercultural, metodología y evaluación de competencias en la comprensión y producción oral en lengua inglesa. Paper presented at the *II Jornada de Reflexión sobre el PIE y el nuevo grado de Estudios Ingleses*. Universitat de València, December 2009.

Clavel Arroitia, B., & Zaragoza Ninet, M. G. (2010). Implementation of an innovation in education project in the degree of English Studies at the University of Valencia. *Portalinguarum, 13*, 103–118.

Fuster Márquez, M., & Clavel Arroitia, B. (2010). Second language vocabulary acquisition and its pedagogical implications. In L. Pérez Ruiz, I. Parrado Román, & P. Tabarés Pérez (Eds.), *Estudios de metodología de la lengua inglesa (V)*. Valladolid: Centro Buendía, Universidad de Valladolid.

Gee, J. P. (1992). *The Social Mind: Language, Ideology and Social Practice*. New York: Bergin & Garvey.

Gregori Signes, C. (2008). Integrating the old and the new: Digital Storytelling in the EFL language classroom. *Greta, 16*, 43–49.

Gregorio Godeo, E. de (2005). Blended-learning as a resource for integrating self-access and traditional face-to face tuition in EFL tertiary education. M-ICTE/2005. Retrieved from http://www.formatex.org/micte2005/110.pdf (01/01/13).

Kiraly, D. (1999). From teacher-centered to learning-centered classrooms in translator education: Control, chaos or collaboration? *Intercultural Studies Group, Online Symposium on Innovation in Translator and Interpreter Training*. Retrieved from http://www.fut.es/~apym/symp/kiraly.html (01/01/2013).

Knowles, M. (1975). *Self-Directed Learning*. Chicago: Follet.

Krashen, S. (1982). *Principles and Practice in Second Language Acquisition*. New York: Pergamon Press.

Mayer, R. (1997). Multimedia learning: Are we asking the right questions? *Educational Psychologist, 32*(1), 1–19.

Mayer, R. (2003). The promise of multimedia learning: Using the same instructional design methods across different media. *Learning and Instruction, 13*(2), 125–139.

Morland, D. V., & Bivens, H. L. (2004). Designing instructional articles in online courses for adult learners. *Innovate Journal of Online Education, 1*(2). Retrieved from http://roi-learning.com/papers/ Designing_Online_Courses-Morland-Bivens-2004.pdf (01/01/13).

Pennock Speck, B. (2009). European convergence and the role of ICT in English Studies at the Universitat de València: Lessons learned and prospects for the future.' In M. L. Pérez Cañado (Ed.), *English Language Teaching in the European Credit Transfer System: Facing the Challenge* (pp. 169–186). Bern/Berlin/Bruxelles/Frankfurt: Peter Lang.

Pennock Speck, B. (2013). Teaching competences through ICTs in an English degree programme in a Spanish setting. In M. L. Pérez Cañado (Ed.), *Competency-based Language Teaching in Higher Education* (pp. 107–118). Amsterdam: Springer.

Pérez Cañado, M. L. (2009) (Ed.). *English Language Teaching in the European Credit Transfer System: Facing the Challenge.* Switzerland: Peter Lang.

Robin, B. R. (2005). Educational Digital Storytelling. Retrieved from http://www.coe.uh.edu/digitalstorytelling/introductiontroduction.htm (01/01/13).
Robin, B. R. (2007). Educational uses of Digital Storytelling. Retrieved from http://www.coe.uh.edu/digital-storytelling/introductiontroduction.htm (01/01/13).

Robin, B. R. (2008). A university/public television collaboration to create and use digital stories to reach audiences in the classroom and beyond. Retrieved from http://faculty.coe.uh.edu/brobin/homepage/University-PublicTelevisionCollaboration.pdf (01/01/13).

Sánchez Sola, A. (2006). El uso de las plataformas telemáticas en las clases presenciales de lengua: El *Internet Classroom Assistant* (ICA). Retrieved from http://espiral.xtec.net/jornada2006/je06_asanchez.pdf (01/01/13).

Seidelhofer, B. (2002). Pedagogy and local learner corpora: Working with learning-driven data. In S. Granger, J. Hung, & S. Petch-Tyson (Eds.), *Computer Learner Corpora, Second Language Acquisition and Foreign Language Teaching* (pp. 213–234). Amsterdam and Philadelphia: John Benjamins.

Sharma, P., & Barrett, B. (2007). *Blended Learning. Using Technology In and Beyond the Language Classroom*. Oxford: Macmillan.

Smith, M. K. (2005). Competence and competencies. *The Encyclopaedia of Informal Education*. Retrieved from http://www.infed.org/biblio/b-comp.htm (01/01/13).

Sweller, J. (1999). *Instructional Design in Technological Areas*. Australia: ACER Press.

Toussaint Clark, C., & Clark, I. (2008). Exploring and exposing the gap in L2 research: How socio-linguistic roles and relationships facilitate or frustrate second language acquisition. *Atlantis. Journal of the Association of Anglo-American Studies, 30*(1), 101–113.

Zaragoza Ninet, M. G., & Clavel Arroitia, B. (2008). ICT implementation in English language and English dialectology. *Greta, 16,* 78–84.

Zaragoza Ninet, M. G. & Clavel Arroitia, B. (2010). Beyond the traditional method: Teaching English with blended-learning methodology. In L. Pérez Ruiz, I. Parrado Román, & P. Tabarés Pérez (Eds.), *Estudios de metodología de la lengua inglesa (V)* (pp. 55–62). Valladolid: Centro Buendía, Universidad de Valladolid.

Aprendizaje Colaborativo Asistido por Ordenador para la Transferencia de las Competencias Mediadora y Lingüístico-comunicativa en Inglés Especializado

Noa Talaván, Elena Bárcena, & Álvaro Villarroel

Abstract

This article describes the process of competence transfer which can take place between different groups of English students undertaking computer supported collaborative language learning, using parameters taken from the Common European Framework of Reference for Languages (Council of Europe, 2001). The students come from two different but related disciplines: the degree in Tourism (where language learning has evident specific purposes within the context of Tourism) and the English-Spanish Translation course from the English Philology degree (where the study of language is an end in itself, with a focus on mediation competence). The article presents an analysis of a collaborative activity of doubling and subtitling (reverse translation from Spanish to English in both cases) of a tourism video (authentic material). This work was undertaken in the context of the CONTACT (Collaborative Network for Translation and Adaptation Activities) project within the Teaching Innovation Network 2009-10 at the UNED (Universidad Nacional de Educación a Distancia/National Distance Education University). The results of this research are presented in terms of the two analytic tools used: namely, scientific observation and evaluation questionnaires. The experience gained in previous collaborative activities has been used to set up this project, which explores the possibilities for the acquisition and interchange of competences related to two different disciplines: English for Tourism and English-Spanish Translation.

Introducción

La enseñanza de lenguas se encuentra en este momento en un periodo de transformación; la revolución en la informática y, especialmente, la generalización en el uso de Internet han propiciado un cambio en la forma y velocidad de transmisión de la información y en las posibilidades de estas herramientas aplicadas a la enseñanza. Por otra parte, en los últimos años se ha acentuado progresivamente la especialización en los saberes, acompañada de la adopción generalizada del inglés como *lingua franca*; esto ha hecho necesario adaptar las técnicas y métodos de enseñanza de inglés a nuevas especialidades profesionales.

Sin embargo, esta "revolución en la lingüística" (Hutchinson y Waters, 1987; Rodgers, 1986) y en la enseñanza de lenguas no es algo que haya surgido ahora de forma aislada, sino que culmina un proceso que se puede considerar que se inició varias décadas atrás. Tras la Segunda Guerra Mundial y el exponencial desarrollo científico, técnico y económico de los países aliados (con los Estados Unidos a la cabeza), las relaciones internacionales se intensificaron, convirtiendo al inglés en el medio de comunicación más común. Como observan estos autores, el inglés se fue consolidando como el idioma internacional del comercio, la investigación y la tecnología y se creó una nueva generación de personas que sabían específicamente por qué y para qué necesitaban el inglés. Entre ellos se encontraban empresarios que necesitaban vender y comprar, ingenieros que necesitaban entender los manuales, médicos que querían estar al tanto de los últimos avances de la medicina, etc. Paralelo al rápido crecimiento en el campo de la ciencia y los descubrimientos científicos, el uso del inglés también se incrementó debido a que los nuevos conceptos necesitaban terminologías actualizadas que sólo existían en esta lengua. Como cada vez más profesionales necesitaban el inglés, surgió inevitablemente la enseñanza del inglés con fines específicos (en adelante, ESP), que se relaciona con una gran variedad de actividades representadas, por ejemplo, en el lenguaje de los ordenadores, las leyes, la terminología de la arquitectura y la medicina, entre muchos otros.

El presente capítulo versa sobre el grado de transferencia de competencias que cabe esperar entre diferentes grupos de estudiantes de lenguas a través del aprendizaje colaborativo (Bárcena, 2011; Richards y Sukwiwat, 2011; Witalisz, 2006), dentro de un proyecto de investigación consistente en el análisis lingüístico y posterior traducción oral y escrita de un texto audiovisual con fines turísticos. Para ser más precisos, en este caso se intenta estudiar la posible transferencia de competencias entre un grupo de estudiantes de una Diplomatura de Turismo, cuyo aprendizaje de la lengua tiene fines específicos, y a la cual darán un uso primordialmente vehicular, y otro grupo de estudiantes de Filología Inglesa, para los cuales el estudio de la lengua es un fin en sí mismo, aunque su interés académico está centrado en la competencia mediadora (Consejo de Europa, 2001). Partimos de una realidad en la que los alumnos de Turismo adquieren las competencias de ESP para dicha área, y desarrollan predominantemente las destrezas propias de su sublenguaje (terminología, etc.) (Varela, 2003). Por su parte, los alumnos de Filología, como cabe esperar, adoptan un enfoque diferente respecto al aprendizaje de la lengua inglesa, profundizando en aspectos gramaticales, semánticos y etimológicos que no forman apenas parte de los estudios de ESP para Turismo. La hipótesis de investigación de este trabajo se basa, pues, en la posibilidad de transferencia de conocimientos entre los alumnos de ambas titulaciones en el contexto de un proyecto de trabajo colaborativo que favorezca este trasvase. Unido a esto, se incluye el uso de una estrategia relativamente nueva para ambos grupos de estudiantes: la traducción audiovisual, en forma de subtitulación y doblaje, para el aprendizaje de lenguas.

Objetivos y marco teórico

El experimento docente que se presenta en las páginas siguientes tiene como objetivo principal la mejora de destrezas lingüísticas específicas mediante aprendizaje colaborativo en dos grupos de alumnos de dos disciplinas diferentes: para los alumnos de Traducción, la competencia mediadora, y para los alumnos de Turismo, la competencia comunicativa en un dominio especializado y destrezas orales (que no habían desarrollado hasta la fecha).

Dado que la hipótesis principal de esta investigación es la transferencia efectiva de competencias entre ambos grupos de alumnos, un segundo objetivo a evaluar se plasma a continuación: mejorar la competencia mediadora (para los estudiantes de Turismo) y mejorar los conocimientos de inglés especializado (para los estudiantes de Traducción). Estos objetivos se pretenden alcanzar dentro de un marco teórico que se integra dentro del enfoque comunicativo de enseñanza de lenguas (Wilkins, 1976) y el Marco Común Europeo de Referencia para las Lenguas (Consejo de Europa, 2001; en adelante, MCER), como marco general de aprendizaje-enseñanza de lenguas.

La comunicación humana está intrínsecamente unida al lenguaje y ambos son naturales del ser humano. Por este motivo, si enseñamos a los alumnos a hablar una lengua o a comprenderla, debemos enseñarles naturalmente, en entornos comunicativos reales, donde ellos puedan tener un papel activo. Así podrán aprender con situaciones familiares y adaptables a su vida cotidiana, y esto es lo que se ha pretendido hacer en este experimento, siguiendo la línea del enfoque comunicativo. Como comenta Littlewood (1992: 106), es necesario que sean los alumnos los que vayan tomando decisiones en lo que respecta a su aprendizaje:

> Adopting active roles implies that the learners make choices and decisions which affect their own learning activity [...] Since using language involves making choices in any case, it is largely a question of extending these choices further up a scale so that, as their course progresses, learners become more and more capable of operating independently both in their communication and in their learning.

Como se podrá comprobar más adelante, los alumnos participantes en este proyecto han tenido un rol totalmente activo y se les ha dejado tomar sus propias decisiones, afectando éstas a su propia actividad de aprendizaje y convirtiéndolos en actantes cada vez más independientes.

En lo que respecta al MCER, este documento ha servido de justificación teórica al desarrollo de la competencia de la mediación y a la utilización de estrategias colaborativas en entornos reales. El MCER recupera la traducción desde el punto de vista de la mediación, como estrategia fundamental a desarrollar dentro de la enseñanza-aprendizaje de lenguas extranjeras. Es cierto que el uso de la traducción presenta algunos inconvenientes en la didáctica de lenguas, ya que no es un proceso comunicativo natural y directo (sólo se centra en dos destrezas: leer y escribir) y por ello algunas personas la ven como una actividad mecánica y de escaso interés, excesivamente centrada en la precisión de la transferencia. Afortunadamente, sus ventajas didácticas también son múltiples, ya que se ha comprobado que la traducción potencia el desarrollo de distintas destrezas, la mejora de los conocimientos lingüísticos y el desarrollo de la competencia cultural, dentro de la enseñanza-aprendizaje de lenguas (Hurtado, 1999). Además, en este caso los alumnos no realizan una traducción en el sentido tradicional de la misma, sino una traducción audiovisual (en adelante, TAV). En la TAV se ha de pasar de dos códigos (textual y visual) a uno solo (textual) y hay que atenerse a unas restricciones de sincronía que la convierten en una actividad más completa y creativa, donde se presta más atención a la esencia del mensaje comunicativo que a las expresiones y estructuras lingüísticas de un modo más aislado y abstracto (Talaván, 2010).

Por último, es necesario mencionar otros tres fundamentos metodológicos a tener en cuenta dentro del marco teórico de la presente investigación: la relación de intersección entre las sublenguas de los múltiples dominios que existen en una lengua general, incluida la lengua estándar (Girardot, 2006); la Enseñanza de Lenguas Asistida por Ordenador (ELAO), donde el uso de las TIC posibilita un aprendizaje activo, basado en tareas y centrado en el aprendiz (Cabero, 2007); y el aprendizaje colaborativo, que trata a los estudiantes como seres eminentemente sociales, desde el punto de vista constructivista (Ernest, 1995).

Desarrollo de la investigación

La investigación que se presenta y analiza a continuación está basada en un proyecto colaborativo de doblaje y subtitulación (traducción inversa en ambos casos, del español al inglés) de un video turístico (material real, no educativo). Este proyecto, denominado CONTACT (Collaborative Network for Translation and Adaptation Activities), se desarrolló dentro del programa Redes para la Innovación Docente 2009-10 de la Universidad Nacional de Educación a Distancia (UNED).

El equipo humano que participó en este proyecto fueron 3 administradores (equipo docente) y 15 alumnos (3 grupos de 5 sujetos cada uno), procedentes tanto de los estudios de Turismo (pertenecientes a la asignatura "Lengua Inglesa I"), como de Filología Inglesa (provenientes de la asignatura "Análisis Contrastivo de Textos Inglés-Español", una asignatura de traducción general), a partes aproximadamente iguales. Después de analizar la producción escrita y oral de los sujetos, se pudo concluir que todos ellos pertenecían al nivel B de dominio de la lengua, al que el MCER señala como *usuarios competentes de la lengua.*

Los recursos utilizados fueron los siguientes: la plataforma educativa aLF (como campus virtual propio de la UNED para el estudio y evaluación continua de las materias y también para el intercambio de información); la herramienta de videoconferencia AVIP (que les daba acceso a una comunicación sincrónica global); un texto audiovisual de 5-6 minutos procedente de YouTube-*MuchoViaje.com* (vídeo promocional de la ciudad de Santander); y diversos programas de software libre para subtitular (*Aegisub*), doblar (*Audacity*) y transformar el vídeo (*A Tube Catcher*).

La plataforma aLF (www.innova.uned.es/dotlrn) es una plataforma de e-Learning y colaboración[1] que permite impartir y recibir formación, gestionar y compartir documentos, crear y participar en comunidades temáticas, así como realizar proyectos en línea. aLF comenzó a funcionar en el año 2000, es utilizada por profesorado y alumnado y va evolucionando a medida que evolucionan las aplicaciones informáticas y se atiende a las sugerencias de los usuarios. Como característica principal, aLF facilita hacer un buen uso de los recursos telemáticos a través de Internet para paliar las dificultades que ofrece el modelo de enseñanza a distancia. Para ello, pone a disposición de sus usuarios las herramientas necesarias para que tanto el equipo docente como el alumnado encuentren la manera de compaginar el trabajo individual como el aprendizaje colaborativo (González Boticario y otros, 2010).

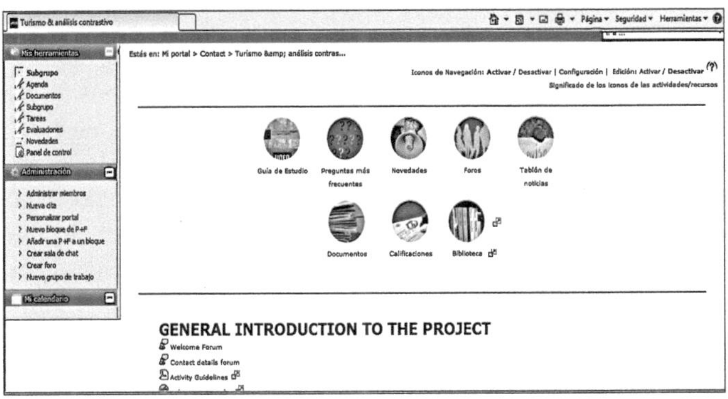

Fig. 1: *Interfaz principal de la comunidad creada en aLF para el proyecto CONTACT*

1 Aunque está desarrollada específicamente para la comunidad de profesorado y alumnado de la UNED, es también parcialmente accesible al público en general.

Asimismo, los alumnos han contado con la posibilidad de utilizar la herramienta de videoconferencia AVIP (*Herramienta AudioVisual sobre tecnología IP*), cuyas aplicaciones van más allá de una mera sala de videoconferencia, con unas instalaciones especialmente preparadas para la docencia, siendo auténticas aulas virtuales con múltiples aplicaciones, que ofrecen una alta calidad de imagen y sonido y cuentan con equipamiento de última generación. Este sistema de videoconferencia se engloba dentro del Plan AVIP de la UNED para interconectar todos sus centros educativos y ofrecer una experiencia de formación de mayor calidad utilizando nueva tecnologías.

Fig. 2: *Imagen de sesión AVIP en CONTACT*

En cuanto al software de subtitulación utilizado, *Aegisub* (www.aegisub.org), se trata de un editor de subtítulos de propósito general que facilita en muchos aspectos la composición tipográfica. Se ha elegido este programa para el proyecto CONTACT, ya que, como se ha indicado, es software libre y además cuenta con características de gran utilidad, como importar subtítulos no Unicode desde más de 30 codificaciones diferentes, lo que permite reanudar el trabajo sobre cualquier subtítulo, independientemente de la configuración del sistema. Además, permite cargar los formatos de subtítulo de varios tipos (.ass, .txt, etc), y también cuenta con resaltado de sintaxis. El manejo de este programa de subtitulación es bastante sencillo e intuitivo, incluso para los no iniciados.

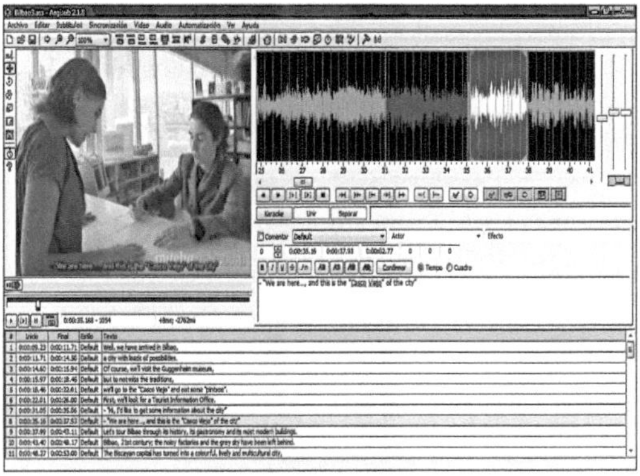

Fig. 3: *Interfaz de Aegisub con subtítulos creados por el alumnado en el proyecto*

Para la selección del texto audiovisual, se tuvo en cuenta que fuera un texto con fines específicos para Turismo, pero se acordó buscar un fragmento de habla que no contuviese una cantidad excesiva de términos profesionales, ni que estuviese dirigido expresamente a profesionales del sector, habida cuenta que los grupos que iban a trabajar con él eran alumnos y, en casi todos los casos, era la primera experiencia de este tipo. En cuanto a la longitud del texto que debía ser traducido y doblado por los alumnos, se estimó como recomendable una duración de entre cinco y diez minutos, con el fin de evitar hacer la tarea más complicada en términos de carga textual (Wagener, 2006): el texto seleccionado finalmente tiene una duración de 6 minutos y consta de 600 palabras aproximadamente. El lenguaje que contiene dicho texto audiovisual es un aspecto igualmente importante; por ello, se consideró que era necesario que tuviera partes proporcionales de narración y diálogo, ya que las técnicas de subtitulación y doblaje son distintas según el tipo de intercambio comunicativo. En la búsqueda de textos audiovisuales de este tipo, se pudo comprobar la tendencia a predominar la narración y por ello se tuvieron que descartar muchos textos, que en otros aspectos se ajustaban al perfil que se buscaba. Tras una selección de varios textos que cumplían los requisitos se optó por utilizar el vídeo promocional de Santander que se mencionó anteriormente: www.youtube.com/watch?v=Z7f6fzwuqZE.[2]

En cuanto al software utilizado para el doblaje, en este caso se optó por elegir *Audacity* (http://audacity.sourceforge.net/?lang=es), una aplicación informát-

2 Cabe destacar que en las encuestas realizadas a los alumnos participantes en el proyecto, cuyos resultados serán analizados en secciones posteriores, el índice de satisfacción referido al texto audiovisual fue muy alto. También hubo varios comentarios en los foros destacando este aspecto.

ica de uso libre que se puede usar para grabación y edición de audio. Se eligió este programa por ser el editor de audio más difundido y por contar con las características necesarias para este proyecto; incluye un editor avanzado de audio con el que se puede cortar, reunir, reducir el tamaño, mezclar, y aplicar efectos y filtros.

En lo que respecta al software de edición de vídeo, los alumnos que participan en esta experiencia de aprendizaje colaborativo necesitaban un programa que les permitiera transformar el texto audiovisual en un archivo de vídeo con el que poder trabajar directamente, ya que el texto que se les propuso se presentó como un link, por lo que tenían que descargar el vídeo personalmente en su ordenador. El programa utilizado con ese fin en el presente proyecto ha sido *a Tube Catcher* (http://atube-catcher.softonic.com/). Este software descarga vídeos de sitios web como YouTube, tiene soporte para más de cien sitios para compartir vídeos; puede descargar contenidos multimedia al ordenador en múltiples formatos (avi., mpeg., mov., etc.), e incluso puede extraer sólo pistas de audio de los vídeos y puede personalizar las opciones y conseguir una mayor calidad de vídeo. Se ha elegido por tratarse de software libre, por ser uno de los más usados y porque tiene una interfaz sencilla de utilizar.

La duración del proceso de investigación fue de diez semanas aproximadamente, y éstas se situaron al final del segundo cuatrimestre, lo que dio tiempo a que los estudiantes estuvieran familiarizados con los demás aspectos del curso, conocieran a sus compañeros, etc. En lo que respecta a las tareas realizadas por los alumnos a lo largo del proceso, éstas se pueden resumir del siguiente modo:

- Primera: todos los alumnos contaban con un periodo inicial de familiarización con la actividad y las herramientas.
- Segunda: los alumnos de Traducción tenían que traducir y subtitular el vídeo con la asistencia de los estudiantes de Turismo, que les debían asesorar a lo largo de la traducción en todo lo concerniente a problemas relativos a vocabulario especializado del área.
- Tercera: los alumnos de Turismo, en una segunda fase, realizaban la traducción para doblaje y posterior grabación de audio en inglés con la asistencia de los estudiantes de Traducción en cualquier aspecto relacionado con problemas de competencia mediadora.
- Cuarta y última: todos los alumnos debían cumplimentar un cuestionario de evaluación sobre la actividad.

Desde el primer momento, los alumnos contaron con una descripción pormenorizada del proceso a seguir en las distintas tareas y se les proporcionaron toda clase de documentos de pasos a seguir, instrucciones y guías de diversa índole, elaborados del modo más claro y sintético posible. Un ejemplo de estas orientaciones y textos se puede ver en la Figura 4, a continuación.

ACTIVITY TIPS

Step by step forum

Remember you need to work with your group (1, 2, 3, or 4). You have your own group space lo upload documents or to discuss in the forum, or even to chat. This general space is for general information and questions.

Step one
Subtitle the clip. You must bear in mind that subtitles are a reduced version of the dialogue, so the translation must be consice, grasping the message and never a word for word translation. You should share the work and maybe work on a paper (word document) draft first, before you create the subtitles.
Each group must decide how to distribute their work.

Step two
Dub the clip. You must bear in mind that translating for dubbing is different. You have more time than for subtitles, so you don't need to be concise. However, if the mouth of the speaker is visible, your translation needs to adapt to his/her mouth movements.
You should share the work and maybe work on a paper (word document) draft first, before you record your audio file. When you record it, watch the clip at the same time as if you were really dubbing it, adjusting your words to the speakers' mouth movements, when they are visible. If not, there is more freedom in the translation.

Dubbing guidelines

Fig. 4: *Extracto de las claves de seguimiento de la actividad en aLF*

Análisis de los resultados

Los resultados de la investigación cualitativa realizada se presentan a continuación a través de las dos herramientas de análisis básicas utilizadas: la monitorización de la actividad y los cuestionarios de evaluación. Desde el punto de vista de la monitorización u observación de la actividad, es necesario hablar del proceso en sí y describir las fases de las que constó la experiencia, por un lado, y del uso de herramientas de trabajo colaborativo, por otro.

La primera fase del proyecto se desarrolló durante la primera semana de las ocho de que constó esta experiencia. El equipo docente preparó las actividades y se realizaron tareas tales como la selección de los programas de software a utilizar, documentos tutoriales de uso de dichos programas, búsqueda y selección de textos audiovisuales adecuados, elaboración de los documentos que se iban a dirigir a los alumnos, planificación de los plazos que deberían cumplir los alumnos y distribución de tareas.

La segunda fase del proyecto (convocatoria, plazos y matriculación de alumnos) se realizó en la segunda semana, así como su distribución en grupos. Como se ha dicho anteriormente, el proyecto se ofertó desde dos asignaturas de dos titulaciones distintas y los alumnos se apuntaron en gran número, siendo necesario cerrar la inscripción antes del plazo previsto. Se pasó entonces a confeccionar los grupos de trabajo. Al ser alumnos provenientes de dos áreas diferentes, se les intentó distribuir proporcionalmente en todos los grupos, algo imprescindible si se quiere analizar nuestra hipótesis principal de investigación:

la posible transferencia de competencias entre diferentes grupos de aprendizaje de lenguas.

La tercera fase consistió en la introducción de los alumnos al proyecto y comienzo del trabajo por grupos. Se desarrolló entre la tercera y quinta semana. Una vez elaborados y colgados los documentos y programas que iban a utilizar los alumnos, facilitados los tutoriales de los mismos y el guión y plazos con los que deberían trabajar, el equipo docente instó a los participantes a registrarse en aLF y, como primera actividad, abrir en el foro de su grupo un hilo de saludo y presentación. Los 4 grupos constituidos inicialmente se formaron del total de 24 alumnos inscritos en el proyecto, si bien ya al inicio se contó con la posibilidad de tener que reducir los grupos en tamaño o en número por la baja participación de algunos de los alumnos. El abandono es una constante en educación a distancia (Carrión, 2005), y tras la primera semana había un número de 8 a 10 alumnos que no se habían incorporado, por lo que se decidió reagrupar los grupos 3 y 4 para formar un solo grupo. Finalmente, quedaron inscritos 15 alumnos en 3 grupos (5 por grupo).

Aproximadamente durante los primeros 10 días surgieron problemas de desorientación en la incorporación al proyecto, dificultades en la comprensión del manejo de algunos programas requeridos, incompatibilidad de los equipos informáticos de alguno de los miembros de los grupo, etc. Durante estos primeros días, la labor del equipo docente tuvo que ser especialmente rápida y eficaz en la respuesta que se daba a los alumnos, de manera que éstos no se vieran envueltos en dificultades insalvables. Al igual que se ha comentado la importancia de realizar bien las tareas de la primera fase del proyecto (preparación, materiales, etc.), este momento del proyecto es vital para que los alumnos se vean apoyados y se involucren en las tareas. Asimismo, durante estos primeros días ya se empezó a observar cómo había alumnos que se involucraban muy activamente en el proyecto, ejerciendo una labor de liderazgo notable.

Superado este breve periodo, los grupos trabajaron de forma autónoma y eficaz, distribuyendo roles entre sus miembros y, consecuentemente, la labor del equipo docente pasó a ser de supervisión del trabajo y resolución de algunas dudas puntuales. En este punto del proyecto, ya se pudieron determinar las claves para que un proyecto colaborativo de estas características tuviera éxito: cálculo de expectativas realistas a la hora de configurar los grupos de trabajo (la inscripción de alumnos superará en un porcentaje alto a los que finalmente acaben involucrándose en el proyecto), cuidado y meticulosidad en la preparación de la información inicial del proyecto (debe ser clara y concisa, pero abundante) y, finalmente, acierto en la elección del texto audiovisual que se va a trabajar, que ha de estar lingüísticamente adaptado al nivel de los alumnos, además de resultar atractivo para ellos.

En general, los grupos trabajaron de forma autónoma siguiendo un modelo creado por ellos mismos. Primero se asignaban tareas entre ellos, intercambiándose documentos y planteándose cuestiones generales a través de los foros. Después se citaban en las salas de chat para tratar asuntos más específicos o tomar decisiones conjuntas sobre aspectos de la traducción, el proceso de subtitulado o el doblaje. Tras la conclusión del plazo dado para entregar el texto audiovisual subtitulado y doblado, se realizó una sesión final conjunta (equipo docente y alumnos) en el aula AVIP. Cada grupo nombró un portavoz que se encargó de presentar su trabajo, así como de hacer una valoración general del proyecto. La sesión fue grabada y puesta a disposición de aquellos que no pudieron asistir en directo. En ella, en general, se plantearon las dificultades que se habían encontrado (más informáticas que lingüísticas), se mostró un alto grado de satisfacción general por haber participado en el proyecto y, en el caso de alguno de los grupos, se reprochó la falta de colaboración de algún compañero.

A modo de análisis global, todos los grupos desarrollaron rápidamente habilidades de trabajo colaborativo tomando como base el principio de que el conocimiento no aparece como algo terminado, sino más bien como una elaboración conjunta que parte de *situaciones-problema*, en donde se elaboran hipótesis, se definen conceptos, se analizan los aspectos involucrados en una situación, se proponen alternativas, se identifican los medios, se evalúan resultados, etc. (Santoyo, 1981), respondiendo, en general, a estas características: interdependencia positiva (que cada miembro del grupo cumpla con sus tareas y que atender la petición de ayuda de los demás es de interés colectivo), responsabilidad individual (cada miembro se considera individualmente responsable de alcanzar la meta del colectivo) e interacción simultánea (que el grupo trabaje en un ambiente psicológico de disponibilidad y mutuo apoyo). Estas tres características se aprecian claramente en los fragmentos de chat analizados, así como en los intercambios de los foros de cada uno de los grupos, y fueron la tónica general en todos los grupos durante el desarrollo del proyecto.

En lo que respecta al segundo aspecto a analizar de la observación de la actividad –el uso de las herramientas de aprendizaje colaborativo–, la plataforma aLF, que se ha utilizado para llevar a cabo CONTACT, cuenta con una serie de aplicaciones. Durante el proyecto, se recogieron datos de participación de los alumnos y de utilización de las diferentes herramientas y, tras la finalización del proyecto, se realizó un análisis que ofrece los siguientes datos de uso de las aplicaciones, donde resultan de especial interés los foros, las carpetas de documentos, las salas de chat y la videoconferencia.

Paquete ≑	Accesos ▾	Minutos ≑
uforums	4953	1071
dotlrn	4622	722
file-storage	1302	1209
file_viewed	344	2154
calendar	127	2
news	29	13
chat	6	1
evaluation	5	1
faq	2	0
bulk-mail	1	0

Fig. 5: *Estadísticas del uso de las herramientas de aLF en la comunidad creada para CONTACT*

Como se puede apreciar en la figura anterior, el uso de las aplicaciones ha sido desigual, constituyendo los foros la principal herramienta que han utilizado los alumnos. En los foros, se han abierto progresivamente, y en todos los grupos, diferentes hilos sobre los temas que iban surgiendo a medida que se avanzaba en el proyecto. Durante las ocho semanas de duración de CONTACT, la participación de los alumnos fue variable, hecho que no debe sorprender en proyectos de aprendizaje colaborativo. La variabilidad en este aspecto es una carencia bastante común en los grupos de aprendizaje colaborativo (Carrión, 2005). No es suficiente con juntar a los estudiantes esperando que sus experiencias previas les proporcionen todo lo necesario para trabajar bien en equipo. En este sentido, es fundamental la formación de la *competencia social* y la madurez de los estudiantes en este plano, aunque es inevitable que se aprecie un índice de variabilidad de unos sujetos a otros. Más allá del inconveniente que supone esta disparidad en la participación, una de las mayores ventajas de los foros es que permite una gran flexibilidad en los tiempos (por su naturaleza asincrónica), aunque también requiere un chequeo y actualización frecuentes. Los temas de los hilos han sido variados, y también lo ha sido la extensión de los mismos, con entradas que varían desde 1 hasta 35 entradas por hilo. Sin embargo, en aquellos casos en los que se necesitaba tomar decisiones de manera rápida y sincrónica, los alumnos han recurrido a las salas de chat o a la videoconferencia (en menor medida).

El uso de las carpetas de documentos (*file-storage*) ha sido bastante extendido y ha funcionado en diferentes direcciones: alumno-alumno, equipo docente-alumno, alumno-equipo docente. El almacenamiento de documentos entre alumnos ha consistido en su mayoría de las sucesivas versiones de las distintas partes (voces) del doblaje (archivos de audio) y de las propuestas de traducciones escritas de cada miembro del grupo, además del archivo/s de subtitulación. La gran ventaja de esta herramienta de almacenamiento de documentos es que permite poner a disposición de los alumnos archivos de gran volumen y almacenarlos durante el tiempo que dure el proyecto. Estas carpetas de documentos también fueron un vehículo de comunicación entre los administradores del proyecto y los alumnos, mediante el cual se facilitaban documentos específicos, como los cuestionarios, las instrucciones, los programas a utilizar, etc.

La utilización de las salas de chat ha sido a demanda de los propios usuarios dentro de cada grupo. En la mayor parte de las ocasiones, los mismos temas tratados en los foros durante varios días generaban debate y éste se trasladaba a una sesión de chat en un horario acordado por todos. La frecuencia de estas reuniones ha variado según los subgrupos de una a dos por semana. En las más de cien páginas que se han recogido de transcripciones de los chats de todos los grupos, se han tratado fundamentalmente temas técnicos de la traducción escrita, la subtitulación y el doblaje, aunque también ha existido debate acerca de aspectos de funcionamiento de los grupos y el reparto de tareas. Los chats incluso han cumplido cierta labor social y de contacto personal de los miembros del grupo, y han servido como vehículo de expresión emociones y de estados de ánimo. Esta herramienta ha contribuido muy eficazmente, a juicio del equipo docente, a cohesionar los grupos y a que los miembros de cada uno de ellos se proporcionasen el apoyo mutuo necesario en momentos de dificultad.

La videoconferencia, por su parte, ha sido un recurso poco utilizado dentro de la plataforma aLF. Sin embargo, su uso fuera de la plataforma ha sido bastante extendido, a juzgar por los comentarios recogidos en los foros. La razón de esta preferencia puede residir en la familiaridad en el uso o la manejabilidad de programas como *Skype*, frente a la herramienta de videoconferencia ofrecida por aLF. Obviamente, estas sesiones han escapado al control de los administradores del proyecto y no existen datos concretos del uso de programas de videoconferencia ajenos a aLF. Sin embargo, cabe destacar la utilidad del uso de videoconferencia en sala AVIP para la sesión final del curso, ya que ésta quedó grabada, especialmente para aquellos alumnos que no pudieron acudir en directo. La sesión fue coordinada por uno de los miembros del equipo docente y a ella asistió un representante de cada uno de los grupos; cada uno de ellos dio su opinión y valoró los aspectos más destacables del proyecto. Globalmente, hubo una valoración general positiva del proyecto, enfatizando las dificultades a la hora de trabajar a distancia con medios técnicos y destacando lo positivo de trabajar de forma colaborativa con otros alumnos (algunos de los cuales no procedían de su misma asignatura). Las opiniones vertidas en esta sesión coincidieron con las expresadas en los cuestionarios acerca del proyecto (que analizaremos en el siguiente punto de este trabajo), proporcionando un mayor grado de fiabilidad a las conclusiones de los mismos.

Los cuestionarios, la segunda herramienta de investigación utilizada, se administraron al total de los 15 alumnos involucrados en la actividad al finalizar el proyecto, por lo que los resultados de los mismos pueden considerarse plenamente relevantes. Las encuestas se dividieron en dos partes: una de datos personales generales y otra de datos específicos del proyecto.

Durante la primera parte de la encuesta, pues, se realizaron una serie de preguntas de carácter personal destinadas a obtener una descripción de la muestra, entre las que cabe destacar el sexo, la procedencia regional y la edad. En lo que se refiere al sexo de los participantes en el proyecto, la mayoría de mujeres sobre varones es clara, de la misma forma que lo es en la matriculación general de ambas carreras que participan en el proyecto: Turismo y Filología Inglesa. No hay, por lo tanto, en un principio, ningún aspecto a destacar en cuanto a su preferencia por la participación en proyectos colaborativos de lenguas de un sexo sobre otro. En cuanto a la procedencia por comunidades autónomas, la dispersión geográfica es bastante grande, siendo Cataluña y Madrid las comunidades que más alumnos aportan al proyecto. Cabe destacar que ningún alumno de la UNED que cursara la carrera desde países extranjeros se incorporó al proyecto; sí participaron en el proyecto dos alumnos extranjeros pero desde sus lugares de residencia en España. Estos resultados se corresponden con la distribución de población por comunidades en España (Madrid y Cataluña), por lo que tampoco resulta un aspecto destacable. Con respecto a las edades de los alumnos, éstas van desde los 25 a los 50 años. Esta dispersión de grupos de edad es también una característica común dentro de la educación universitaria a distancia. En la UNED, y según estudios publicados en base al curso 2005/06, dos de cada tres estudiantes pertenecían a esta franja de edad (Elgarresta, 2006). Esta heterogeneidad no parece que haya supuesto ningún problema para el trabajo de los grupos en CONTACT. Más bien puede haber sucedido todo lo contrario; es decir, los miembros de los grupos, con diferentes edades, se han beneficiados mutuamente y han aportado experiencias y saberes propios de cada edad. Por ejemplo, ante dudas de carácter técnico o informático, se tendía a recibir el consejo de los más jóvenes del proyecto.

En otra sección diferente del cuestionario, más relevante desde el punto de vista de la evaluación de la investigación, preguntados los alumnos por el nivel de inglés, la mayor parte de ellos consideraron que su nivel de inglés era bueno o muy bueno, solamente considerando dos de ellos que su nivel era aceptable (ambos procedentes de la Diplomatura de Turismo).

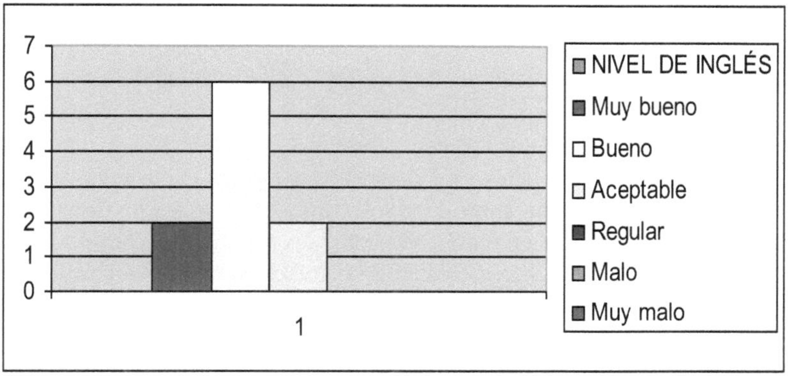

Fig. 6: Nivel de inglés de los participantes en el proyecto

En efecto, el nivel de inglés del colectivo de estudiantes de Turismo suele ser más bajo que el de los estudiantes de Filología Inglesa, teniendo en cuenta que para estos últimos el propio idioma es el objeto principal de los estudios, mientras que los alumnos de Turismo sólo hacen un uso vehicular del mismo. No obstante, en el subconjunto de individuos que realizaron este proyecto, las diferencias no han sido muy acusadas, ya que parece ser que sólo aquellos alumnos de Turismo con cierta confianza en su destreza lingüística comunicativa se prestaron a participar en CONTACT. En este punto, cabe destacar que en la mayoría de casos de encuestas de autoevaluación del nivel de inglés, las respuestas tienden a situarse en un nivel intermedio, siendo poco aclaradoras para quien realiza el cuestionario, o quienes las realizan suelen tener una percepción al alza e su nivel de inglés, superior en muchos casos a la percepción que tienen sus propios profesores (Maíz, 2008). Sin embargo, en esta ocasión, los resultados aportados por los propios alumnos, aunque subjetivos, coinciden con la apreciación que se tiene tras observar su nivel de inglés escrito (foros y chat) y de inglés oral (videoconferencia).

En otro orden de ideas, en dos preguntas separadas se preguntó a los alumnos por la frecuencia de uso de materiales de inglés orales y escritos. En mayor o menor medida, todos afirmaron hacer un uso constante de estos materiales, aunque en las respuestas al cuestionario, se apreció que el uso de materiales escritos es más frecuente que el de materiales orales. Sin duda, la aparición de internet ha facilitado enormemente el acceso a materiales en lengua inglesa (periódicos, revistas on-line, vídeos, etc.), a los que anteriormente había un acceso más restringido. Esta información denota que los alumnos que han participado en el proyecto han tenido de forma regular contacto con materiales en inglés y que, de alguna manera, el inglés ya formaba parte de su tiempo de ocio en forma de lecturas, películas, etc. Este hecho se considera significativo a la hora de enfrentarse a un proyecto de traducción audiovisual (que incluye tanto canales escritos como orales) porque los alumnos iniciaban el proyecto con conocimientos previos y elementos comparativos muy valiosos.

También se instó a los sujetos en el cuestionario a que expusieran las expectativas de mejora que tenían antes de involucrarse en el proyecto; éstas resultaron ser bastante altas tanto en inglés oral como escrito. Es destacable su predisposición a valorar el aprendizaje colaborativo como una forma valiosa de mejorar sus destrezas en la lengua desde antes de comenzar CONTACT. Otra sección del cuestionario preguntaba acerca de la opinión general de los alumnos al finalizar el proyecto; ésta fue, sin duda alguna, positiva. En aprendizaje colaborativo, es especialmente importante la actitud de los alumnos ante las tareas a desarrollar, ya que se trata de un aprendizaje que no está tan sujeto al control de los profesores como otros modos más tradicionales, por lo que es necesario que los participantes en los proyectos tengan un alto nivel de autonomía y de motivación. Por último, se les preguntó respecto a las dificultades que habían encontrado a lo largo del desarrollo del proyecto. Las respuestas de los alumnos son bastante uniformes, y cabe destacar lo positivo de las respuestas referidas al trabajo en los grupos, especialmente en lo que respecta a la facilidad y rapidez en la respuesta de los compañeros, dos aspectos que necesariamente han de funcionar en cualquier experiencia de aprendizaje colaborativo. Los aspectos menos valorados son los referentes al uso de los programas informáticos a disposición de los alumnos, como se puede apreciar en la Figura 7 a continuación.

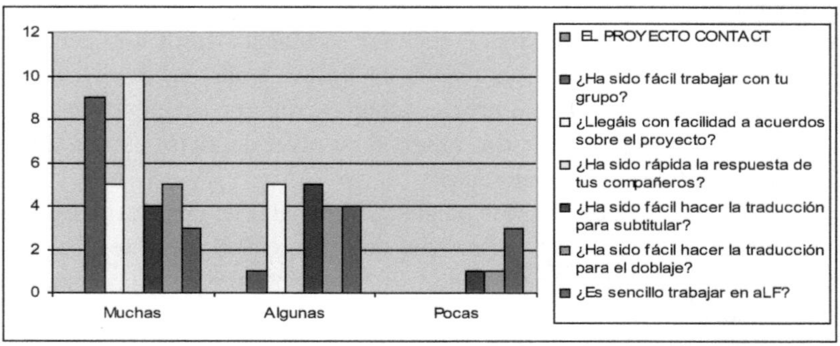

Fig. 7: *Resumen de respuestas de los sujetos en cuanto a posibles dificultadas encontradas*

En el gráfico anterior puede apreciarse como elementos destacables la valoración de los alumnos en cuanto a la facilidad para trabajar con el grupo, la rapidez de la respuesta por parte del equipo docente ante sus dificultades y las escasas dificultades con los medios técnicos.

A modo de resumen de los resultados de los cuestionarios, se pueden proporcionar los siguientes cinco datos significativos: primero, existió una opinión positiva generalizada sobre el proyecto (el 100% de los sujetos repetiría la experiencia); segundo, CONTACT constituyó una introducción positiva al trabajo colaborativo (el 70% de los alumnos no había participado en actividades de aprendizaje colaborativo); tercero, la totalidad de los alumnos considera que ha habido mejoría en sus destrezas traductoras y de expresión en el inglés general y de turismo; cuarto, desafortunadamente, la mejora en recepción oral no fue tan evidente, lo cual es lógico, dado que el texto original estaba en castellano y la mayoría de los intercambios entre alumnos se hicieron por escrito; y quinto y último, el 20% de los alumnos considera que es una actividad que consume gran cantidad de tiempo (esto, en un principio, viene dado probablemente por el gran peso de las TIC en el desarrollo de todas las actividades).

Conclusiones

A lo largo de este capítulo, se ha presentado una experiencia de aprendizaje colaborativo destinada a la transmisión de competencias entre alumnos de distintas áreas y se ha demostrado que, efectivamente, existe dicha transferencia entre los dos grupos de alumnos participantes en el proyecto provenientes de dos titulaciones diferentes.

Lo novedoso de esta investigación cualitativa ha sido aprovechar la experiencia adquirida en anteriores actividades de aprendizaje colaborativo y ponerlo al servicio de un proyecto que busca la adquisición de destrezas propias de dos disciplinas diferentes con la ayuda del potencial pedagógico de la TAV. Se ha pretendido demostrar que es posible el aprendizaje recíproco entre alumnos de disciplinas diferentes a través de un proyecto de aprendizaje colaborativo bien diseñado. Los proyectos de aprendizaje colaborativo de los que se tenía constancia hasta el momento se habían dado entre alumnos involucrados en estudios de la misma disciplina; sin embargo, en este caso se ha buscado desarrollar el aprendizaje entre disciplinas diferentes a través de otra extraña para ambos grupos (TAV), pudiendo así beneficiarse los alumnos de aprendizajes mutuos en diversas direcciones. Si consideramos como probada la hipótesis de investigación sobre la que se basa este trabajo, es decir, que puede existir transferencia de competencias entre alumnos de disciplinas diferentes que se tornan complementarias a través de proyectos de aprendizaje colaborativo llevados a cabo con rigurosidad, el campo que se abre a la enseñanza de lenguas y, en un sentido más amplio, a la enseñanza en general, es muy extenso.

En el desarrollo del proyecto se han diseñado las tareas de tal manera que los alumnos de Filología Inglesa se ocupasen de las tareas más orientadas hacia la lingüística (traducción de textos escritos dirigida a la subtitulación posterior) y que los alumnos de Turismo les ayudaran con temas de vocabulario especializado. Los alumnos de Turismo, por su parte, se encargaban de las tareas con más aspectos de la tarea del doblaje (para desarrollar destrezas orales), mientras que aquí los alumnos de Filología les ayudaban con problemas de mediación que tendían a aparecer en la traducción escrita previa para doblaje. Por lo tanto, en realidad, los alumnos de ambas disciplinas han trabajado de manera indistinta en prácticamente todas las actividades que se les han propuesto, aunque se ha percibido que obviamente el criterio de los alumnos más expertos en una determinada materia se terminaba imponiendo en las decisiones relativas a esa materia. Este proceso se ha repetido de forma natural a lo largo de todo el proyecto y es ahí donde se ha producido una transferencia de competencias: los alumnos de Turismo han aprendido a trabajar desde la lingüística aplicada a la traducción y los alumnos de Filología han profundizado en el campo específico del Turismo. En cuanto a en qué medida se ha producido esa transferencia de competencias, la respuesta no puede ser sencilla, puesto que no se puede cuantificar la adquisición de destrezas de forma exacta en una investigación de estas características.

Como es lógico, existen algunos aspectos de mejora de cara a futuros proyectos. El primero tiene que ver con los plazos de ejecución del proyecto. A juicio de los observadores de la investigación (el equipo docente), y a tenor de los comentarios de algunos de los alumnos, en el caso de un nuevo proyecto, se debería buscar adelantar las fechas de su realización con respecto a las del presente. El desarrollo de un proyecto de estas características durante los meses de abril y mayo presenta algunos inconvenientes; durante estos meses, los alumnos incrementan su carga de trabajo y es difícil para ellos seguir el ritmo de un proyecto de este tipo. Aunque no existen datos comparativos con proyectos similares en diferentes fechas, las opiniones recogidas indican que el abandono (de 24 inscritos inicialmente, sólo realizaron finalmente la actividad 15), siempre alto en educación a distancia, podría haberse reducido en el caso de haberse realizado en fechas anteriores. Otro aspecto que podría intentar mejorarse es la valoración de su participación en el proyecto de cara a la nota final en sus asignaturas; el porcentaje que ha representado este proyecto en el global de la nota de ambas asignaturas ha sido del 5%. Incrementar este porcentaje, sin duda, redundaría en un mayor compromiso por parte de los alumnos con el proyecto y reduciría también el abandono. Asimismo, se podría intentar diseñar futuros proyectos a base de incrementar el número de participantes, bien incluyendo alumnos de otros cursos o incluso de especialidades diferentes. Ampliar el espectro de estudio, sin duda, incrementaría la fiabilidad de los resultados obtenidos. Con todo ello, los autores del presente estudio consideran que este proyecto de aprendizaje colaborativo y los estudios a él asociados deberían continuar en el futuro, no sólo ampliando numéricamente los grupos de sujetos sino fundamentalmente diversificando las materias, para explorar la transferencia de nuevas competencias relacionadas con el lenguaje y la comunicación social.

Bibliografía

Bárcena, E. (2011). Reflexiones sobre el aprendizaje autónomo y social de lenguas extranjeras usando tecnología informática. *CDL Madrid – Revista del Ilustre Colegio de Doctores y Licenciados en Filosofía y Letras y en Ciencias de la Comunidad de Madrid*, 221, 29-30. Documento disponible en http://www.cdlmadrid.org/cdl/htdocs/boletines/ultimo/ultimo.pdf (01/01/13).

Cabero, J. (2007). *Nuevas tecnologías aplicadas a la educación*. Madrid: McGraw-Hill.

Carrión, J. (2005). Una mirada crítica a la enseñanza a distancia. *Revista Iberoamericana de Educación*, 36. Documento disponible en http://www.rieoei.org/deloslectores/11Carrion.pdf (01/01/13).

Consejo de Europa (2001). *Common European Framework of Reference for Languages: Learning, Teaching, Assessment*. Cambridge: Cambridge University Press.

Elgarresta, J. A. (2006). La UNED se pone el mono de trabajo. *La Verdad Digital*, 9 de octubre de 2006. Documento disponible en http://www.laverdad.es/.

Ernest, P. (1995). The one and the many. En L. Steffey y J. Gale (Eds.), *Constructivism in Education* (pp. 459-486). Nueva Jersey: Lawrence Erlbaum Associates.

Girardot, L. (2006). Formación docente en Inglés con Fines Específicos. *Acción Pedagógica, 15*(1), 74-82.

González Boticario, J., Gaudioso, E. y Hernández del Olmo, F. (2000). Una organización de los recursos de internet para la enseñanza a distancia. *Revista Iberoamericana de Educación a Distancia, 3*, 51-73.

Hurtado, A. (1999). *Enseñar a traducir. Metodología en la formación de traductores e intérpretes. Teoría y fichas prácticas*. Madrid: Edelsa.

Hutchinson, T. y Waters, A. (1987). *English for Specific Purposes: A Learning Centered Approach*. Cambridge: Cambridge University Press.

Littlewood, W. (1992). *Teaching Oral Communication: A Methodological Framework*. Oxford: Blackwell.

Maíz, C. (2008). Aprendiendo a aprender: Técnicas de auto-evaluación en el aula de inglés. *Revista Pulso, 31*, 161-180.

Richards, J. C. y Sukwiwat, M. (2011). Language transfer and conversational competence. *Applied Linguistics 32*(1), 1-13.

Rodgers, T. (1986). *Approaches and Methods in Language Teaching*. Cambridge: Cambridge University Press.

Santoyo, R. (1981). Algunas reflexiones sobre la coordinación en los grupos de aprendizaje. *Perfiles Educativos*, *118*, 3-19.

Talaván, N. (2010). Subtitling as a task and subtitles as support: Pedagogical Applications. En J. Díaz-Cintas, A. Matamala y J. Neves (Eds.), *New Insights into Audiovisual Translation and Media Accessibility* (pp. 285-299). Amsterdam: Rodopi.

Varela, R. (2003). *Communicative Situations in Tourism*. Madrid: Editorial Universitaria Ramón Areces.

Wagener, D. (2006). Promoting independent learning skills using video on digital language laboratories. *Computer Assisted Language Learning*, *19*, 279-286.

Wilkins, D. A. (1976). *Notional Syllabuses: A Taxonomy and Its Relevance to Foreign Language Curriculum Development*. Oxford: Oxford University Press.

Witalisz, E. (2006). Transfer in L2 writing: Linguistic competence vs. composing skills. *Studia Linguistica*, *123*, 1-10.

An Innovative Approach for Developing Oral Skills in English in a Distance Course

Pilar Rodríguez-Arancón & María Jordano-de la Torre

Abstract

One of the greatest difficulties encountered by our students at the UNED (Universidad Nacional de Educación a Distancia/National Distance Education University) is the development of comprehension and production skills in English. Although our courses are designed taking into account all the peculiarities of our students, it is difficult to create activities which will help promote greater comprehension and more fluency in a second language when teacher-student interaction, or even interaction among students, is not the norm.

This paper presents an innovative way in which this problem has been addressed in *Contact*, one of the projects carried out as part of the Networks for Teaching Innovation of the UNED. The aim of the project was to get our students to work in collaboration with individuals from other nationalities, with only English as a Second Language in common, and for them to create routes for travelling around different areas of the world.

Most of the conversations generated, whether in small or large groups, were recorded so that they could be studied from a multimodal perspective. Final surveys were also required in order to ascertain the level of achievement attained by the participants, and also to pinpoint the strong and weak aspects of the project.

1 Introduction

Working and studying in a distance education setting implies many unique aspects apart from the obvious difficulties arising from the geographical distances. The UNED is a complex institution, with centres all over the world. It strives to develop new ideas which can help our students to learn and our work as teachers to be more productive and thorough. One such initiative is offered yearly with the funding of the projects within the Networks for Teaching Innovation. Contact was one of the projects carried out in the academic year 2009/10.

Contact is the result of an effort to bring together students of different ages, interests, levels of English and ICT, and with different time commitments. The aim of the project was to get our students to work on a project using only the English language to communicate. The students were divided into three different groups, each of which was in charge of a route. They had to design a tour around their specific area of the world and gather information about places of interest, accommodation, custom regulations, etc. by communicating with foreign students from that area and then by doing some more research within their own groups.

All the students had to take part in a final presentation of the information gathered. One person from each of the three groups was also responsible for recording all the conversations between foreign and UNED students, as well as among UNED students themselves, which was done using Skype technology and, as pointed out above, always in English. Finally, satisfaction questionnaires were also created to highlight the level of achievement attained by the participants, and to pinpoint the strong and weak aspects of the proposal.

Our aim was of special significance as the spoken competence was a particularly neglected skill at the beginning of the development of the Distance Learning of Languages (DLL). However, thanks to the work of its fourth generation (Jung, 2005; Thorpe, 1998; Wang & Sun, 2001) and the continuous development of Voice over Internet Protocol (VoIP) tools, practicing and assessing spoken skills at a distance is now possible. Due to this technological revolution, not only in DLL but in English Language Teaching (ELT) in general, the current trend of Computer Assisted Language Learning (CALL) has also experienced a change of direction, moving into Computer Mediated Communication (CMC) studies.

2 Synchronous Computer Mediated Communication studies (SCMC)

Since the Internet appeared for the first time in the language teaching area in the 1990s, in what was called the third Distance Learning generation (Boyle, 1995; Garrison, 1985; Thorpe, 1998; Wang & Sun, 2001), CMC has been acquiring importance year by year. It achieved such relevance that the Journal of Computer of Computed Mediated Communication was created in 1995 as an online publishing service. One decade later, a special interest group called CMC SIG emerged from the EuroCALL Association to disseminate the research carried out in the area. As a result of these two facts, as well as of several publications on this topic, CMC can now be considered as a body of knowledge in its own right. Close to it in nature, we can find intercultural studies generated online (Belz, 2003; Breeze, 2003; Liaw & Bunn-Le Master, 2010; O'Dowd, 2007; Scarino, 2008). This is a crucial point to take into account when dealing with Tourism and English for Specific Purposes (ESP) studies, such as the research presented in this paper.

SCMC research has been studied from several perspectives:

- Negotiation of meaning (Schwienhorst, 2004; Wang, 2006)
- Discourse study and conversational analysis (Bower & Hedberg, 2010; Enriquez, 2009; Lamy, 2004; O'Rourke, 2008; Sauro, 2004; Tudini, 2005).
- Intercultural perspective (Liaw & Bunn-Le Master, 2010; O'Dowd & Waire, 2009; Vinagre & Muñoz, 2011).

- Multimodal perspective (Berglund, 2009; Ciekanski & Chanier, 2008; Hauck & Youngs, 2008; Norris, 2004; Kress & Leeuwen, 2001; Sauro, 2004).
- Task-based orientation (Foster & Tavakoli, 2009; Gilaber, 2007; Hauck & Youngs, 2008; Kessler, 2010; O'Dowd, 2009; Yilmaz & Granena, 2010).
- Fluency and anxiety studies (Kessler, 2010).
- Motivation (Chiu *et al.*, 2007; Raby, 2007; Ransdell, 2010).

Technology advances so quickly that the language generated in a voice chat ten years ago could not possibly be compared with that generated today without bearing in mind certain factors. Thanks to the inclusion of voice in the CMC area of Applied Linguistics studies, Distance Learning and Language Learning in general have experienced a crucial change in the techniques employed. Among the most recent works, we find those produced by authors such as Jaya (2008), Kenning (2010), or Rosell-Aguilar (2005). Egbert & Petrie (2005) mention six different elements to take into account when doing research on CALL, also extremely important when dealing with CMC:

- Learners. In our case, adult students in very special circumstances. Most of them are only part-time students because they have other commitments.
- Language level. It ranges from very low to very high levels.
- Context. Having to struggle with distance learning can be an obstacle on many occasions.
- Tools. Students will use completely new ICT tools in order to perform the tasks proposed during this study.
- Tasks/activities. They have been proposed to work in collaboration according to the Bologna Plan premises and the *Common European Framework of Reference for Languages: Learning, Teaching, Assessment* (CEFR) (Council of Europe, 2001).
- Peers and teachers. They are of course represented by the tutors of this particular course.

Taking into account the different perspectives and factors involved in SCMC, this paper will present a study of the experience carried out focusing on a multimodal analysis of some of the most relevant interventions of the students, complemented by the results of a qualitative survey delivered to the students at the end of the practice. Jones (2004) considers the context in CMC as something to be studied from a multimodal point of view, since it helps to understand and study the language generated better. He distinguishes different dichotomies that separate the virtual from the real, the sender from the receiver, the public from the private, the figure from the ground and the text from the context.

3 Research context

3.1 Some data about the institution

The Universidad Nacional de Educación a Distancia/National Distance Education University (UNED) was created in Madrid (Spain) in 1972. It grew quickly into two different areas of Humanities and Sciences and it has developed greatly from its beginnings of free posting of study units to the students of 80 local centres around the world, catering for more than 200,000 students, 4,000 of whom suffer some kind of disability and around 1,500 of whom belong to special prison programmes. In the 1990s, new technologies started to be implemented, and the application of multimedia systems provided not only the creation of teaching materials, but also their distribution. It is now the largest university in Spain and offers 26 degree courses, over 500 training courses and relies on over 10,000 people working distributed among the central buildings in Madrid and the local centres.

With these figures, it is clear that teaching and learning are radically different from the environment offered in any other university in Spain or even in Europe, so special methods were devised to help students achieve their study goals successfully. Thanks to projects like Networks for Teaching Innovation, teachers, tutors and students receive support to improve their teaching and learning both via funding and also via academic tokens, so that the resulting outcome can be presented in international conferences and scientific articles. This provides an extra motivation for the participants in the project, since most of the students share a lack of time for their studies as a consequence of family and work commitments.

3.2 The participants

The 29 students involved in this project (out of a possible number of over 2,000) came from two different subjects: English for Tourism I and English for Specific Purposes: Business and Law, offered by the Faculties of Economics and Language Studies, respectively, to several degrees. Since there are different degrees involved, interest was also varied. The students decided to take part in the project voluntarily and were given extra points in the score of the final grades at the end of the academic year, plus some extra credits.

The following graph shows the proportion of degrees involved:

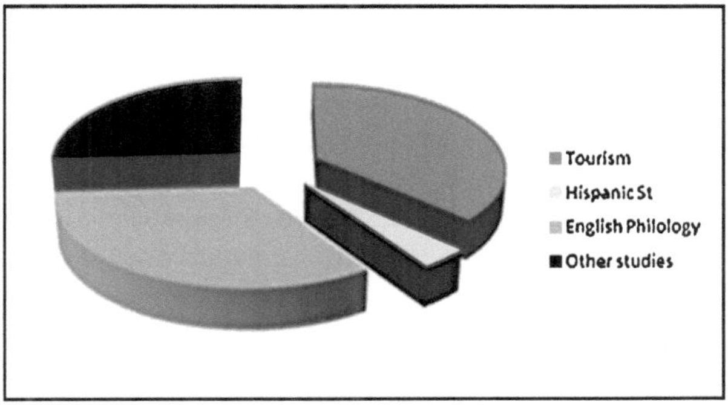

Fig. 1: *Participants' degrees*

As shown in the figure above, most of the participants were students of Tourism or English Studies (English Philology). The rest belonged to other degrees, being enrolled in this subject as free credits.

4 The project

It was divided into three different sections (Route 1: Italy, Turkey and Morocco; Route 2: Colorado, Argentina and Brazil; and Route 3: Russia, Ukraine, Romania, Poland and Belarus) and all the students had to take part in a final presentation of the information gathered. One person from each of the three groups was responsible for recording all the conversations between foreign and UNED students, as well as among UNED students themselves, which took place using Skype technology. Finally, satisfaction questionnaires were also created to highlight the level of achievement attained by the participants, and also to pinpoint the strong and weak aspects of the proposal.

4.1 Aims

There were several aims in our project; however, the main one was the development of comprehension and production skills in English, which is one of the greatest difficulties encountered by foreign language students everywhere, and our students at the UNED in particular. Although our courses are designed taking into account all the peculiarities of our students, such as lack of time, busy schedules, disabilities, remoteness, etc., it is difficult to create activities which will help promote greater comprehension and more fluency in a second language when teacher-student interaction or even interaction among students is not the norm. Our students dedicate very different times of the day to their courses and also very different amounts of time depending on their daily routines. It is hard to find moments when effective synchronic communication can take place during average working hours. Asynchronous communication is encouraged, but the act of leaving recorded messages for someone else to listen to and answer at a later time cannot really be considered as natural immediate exchanges; and although very positive, there is still a need for simultaneous interaction which implies a continuous adjustment to the evolving patterns of the exchange.

Another important aspect we took into consideration was the opportunity to interact with people from other nationalities, whose first language is not necessarily English. In this way, all communication had to take part in this second language. Thus, all the people involved were working together and developing collaborative skills at the same time as meeting new cultures. Even having to consider the added complications of other time zones to be able to communicate synchronically with team-mates in order to gather information or to present the final stage of the project proved to be fruitful.

Learning the language as well as having the opportunity to relate to people from different cultural backgrounds promotes respect, understanding and tolerance, which are strongly encouraged by the CEFR. The CEFR is the most widely accepted reference for language pedagogy nowadays. It is the culmination of the work on language policy undertaken by the Council of Europe since its very beginning, and is increasingly influencing the learning of languages in European countries. It provides the foundations for a clear definition of teaching and learning objectives and curricular strategies, and the necessary tools for proficiency assessment. Behind this document is the widespread functional and communicative perspective of human language. It follows an action-oriented approach (where learning is seen as an active personal experience and reinterpretation process), which takes into account environmental, cognitive, volitional and emotional resources, as well as the abilities specific to a learner as an individual and a social agent.

As previously mentioned, the students obtained extra scoring in their final qualifications as encouragement and reward for the increased amount of work done in the subject by voluntarily taking part in this project.

4.2 Stages

Contact had four stages of work. In the first one, which took place during the month of January, UNED students and non-UNED volunteers were asked to take part in the project. Our students had a message posted to them in the virtual courses of the afore-mentioned subjects which they were taking. Non-UNED students were selected from different student databases dealing with teaching and learning languages with technologies.

The following graph shows the different nationalities of the students who took part in the experience:

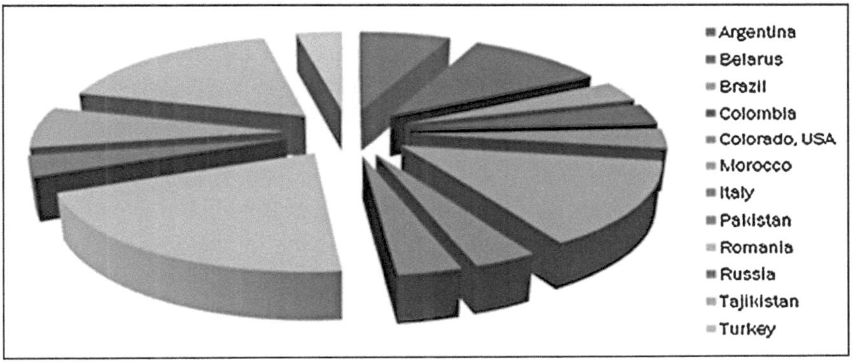

Fig. 2: *Nationalities involved*

During the second phase in February, the groups were organised in three geographical areas according to the residence of the non-UNED language student volunteers. They were joined by a number of UNED students from the group which replied to the message posted by the teachers with a request to participate in the research to be carried out as part of Contact and who freely choose from the different routes available. Later, in the third phase, which ran from the end of February to the end of March, the students went through controlled and uncontrolled working sessions. Some of these sessions were held in small groups, whilst others included all the students working on that particular route. In the last phase in May, the students presented the research they had carried out to the other groups and the teachers.

The research group created a course with access for only those working on the project and also called Contact. The course was designed using aLF, one of the two teaching platforms at UNED. Within it, communication was possible at a general level and group/route level using forums and email.

Throughout all the phases, AVIP (Audiovisual tool with IP technology) weekly sessions took place with the participation of all the students and teachers who could attend at the time determined. The time and the day of the week of the sessions varied in order to try to adjust to the different availabilities of the students. AVIP is a videoconferencing system which allows teachers to talk to students in a certain group, using a digital blackboard and a chat system, and it also records all interventions and presentations for future access.

4.3 Task description

There were a number of short tasks involved in the ongoing process of the investigation. The first one was allocating the students to each of the three groups after which the first synchronous AVIP weekly session took place. There, the students were informed about the work they needed to carry out, which was planning a touristic route around the area corresponding to their individual group (Route 1: Italy, Turkey and Morocco; Route 2: Colorado, Argentina and Brazil; and Route 3: Russia, Ukraine, Romania, Poland and Belarus). The students required assistance from the non-UNED students living in that area by gathering relevant information about places of interest, habits, ways of life, etc. They also received instructions from the teachers through aLF in an asynchronous way. Most of the conversations generated, whether in small or large groups, were recorded so that they could be studied from a multimodal perspective. The conversations were recorded using Skype technology to communicate and exchange information, and Vodburner to record and store them.

The final task in which all participants had to take part was a presentation of the information gathered. It took place in three different sessions dedicated to each of the groups. The topics for the final presentation were:

- Describing places of interest (Tourism students)
- Transport
- Hotels / Resorts
- Costs and expenses of the trips (Business students)
- Custom regulations (Law students)

An image of the recording of one of these sessions can be seen below:

Fig. 3: *Screenshot of one of the sessions*

An evaluation of the process was undertaken by the teachers, following the criteria below for each of the participants. The final scores for their respective subjects were increased and extra credits issued. Final surveys were also designed in order to ascertain the level of achievement attained by the participants, and also to pinpoint the strong and weak aspects of the project.

The following table shows the evaluation criteria used to assess the final works of the participants:

Table 1: *Evaluation criteria*

Item	Maximum Score
Fluency	2
Pronunciation	2
Accuracy	2
Use of specific vocabulary	2
Group coordination	2
Total	10

As shown above, five spoken elements were used to assess the final oral works of the students. The sum of all of them was the final grade.

5 Data and results

In order to set up the whole project, some communication channels were used: virtual course forums (WebCT platform), personal email addresses and a web-based community (dot.lrn based platform, personalized as aLF by the UNED) where all the documents and instructions were provided. Its interface can be seen below:

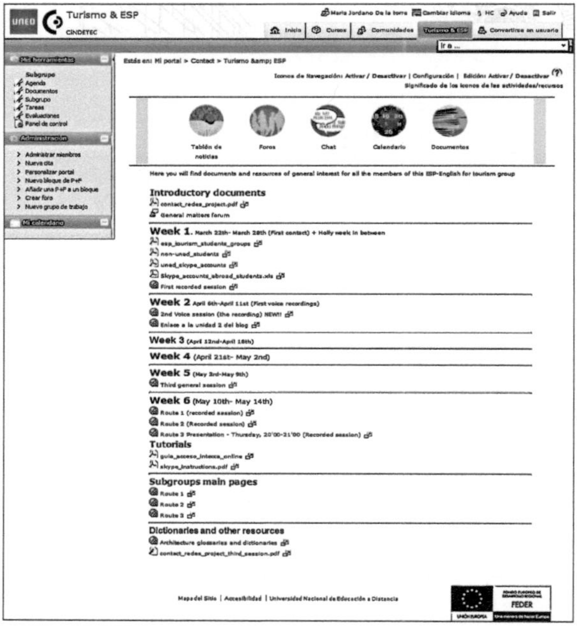

Fig. 4: *aLF Interface*

As can be observed, time was divided into weeks and, during the last week, the presentations of the three groups took place. All of them were recorded and uploaded in the same space for later revision.

5.1 Levels of activity and participation

Apart from the synchronous communication generated via VoIP and Webinars, each of the groups had their own forum, a blog and a moderator. As well as their own group forum, there was a general one for the three groups to discuss general matters.

Some of the most relevant data is shown below:

Table 2: Asynchronous activity

	General community	Route 1	Route 2	Route 3
Sent messages	12	39	115	119
Students Blog (entries)	No blog	1	4 (feelings)	2 (informative)
Number of students involved	27	8	9	10
Student who finished the project	12	3	5	4

The fact that the second group had no moderator, due to external factors, made the chair of this route take on even more protagonism, being the only one who really expressed his desire to continue with the project until finally completed. He even achieved the highest level of participation at the very end of the project. None of the non-UNED students took an active part in the experience, a point that will be commented on later after analysing the results of the survey delivered to the students.

5.2 Multimodal analysis

The following screenshot shows the first general meeting, where most of the participants in the project were present. The session comprised a first part based on a slide presentation with basic instructions about the project, to finish later with questions to the presenter about possible doubts about the work they all had to do.

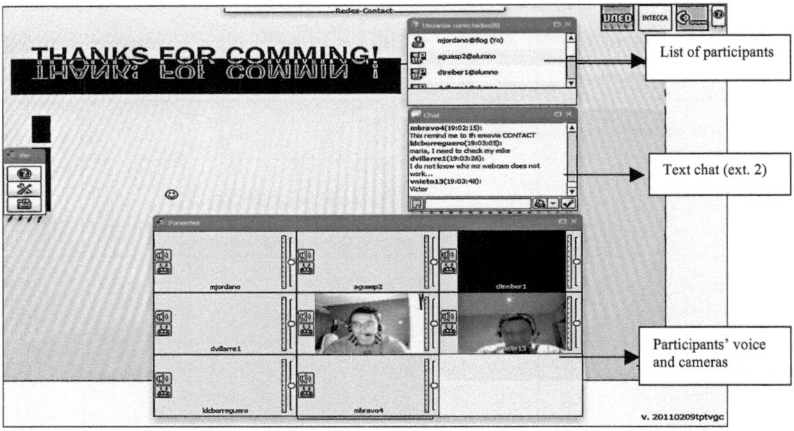

Fig. 5: General session screenshot

Comparing the transcriptions coming from the spoken part and the written one, it is easy to observe how the text chat is characterized by more fluency than the oral one. This could be due to the context, since it was the first time most of the interlocutors had an experience with voice on the Internet.

After the presentation, the moderator gave permission to use voice and cameras to all the audience.
Moderator: Hello!... Now you can speak....Hello! Say Hi! Say
Moderator: Hi Luis! ....Hello!
St4: Can you hear me? Well, I don't know enough… I don't know the name of the group....What's the name of the group?
Moderator: Ah… You are group 1! Are you Dorothee? Yes, you are group 1 or route one, the same.
Moderator: Sorry, My camera doesn't work today. I don't know why.
St4: I don't know what to do know…

Extract 1: Oral transcription. End of first general session

St3(19:00:01): who's second group teacher?
St1(19:00:09): instead of aguaps it could show Alexandra
St4(19:00:14): ok, when I want to enter alf there is a different page than on the demo
St3(19:00:16): so
St5(19:00:44): it is our UNED id
St1(19:00:59): I know...
St3(19:01:17): I want to say hi
St2(19:01:19): I would like to saz hello
St6(19:01:20): hi everyone, it has been a pleasure!
tutor1(19:01:21): Yes, please Maria, I need to check my mike

St5(19:02:15): This remind me to th emovie CONTACT
tutor1(19:03:05): Maria, I need to check my mike
St2(19:03:26): I do not know whz mz webcam does not work...
St3(19:03:48): Victor
St5(19:03:58): this is getting slower are more cameras are connected
St6(19:04:14): My camera is working and I do not how I got it
St5(19:04:33): Good bye

Extract 2: Text chat. End of first general session

As can be seen from extract 2, there are fewer silent moments than in extract 1 and more participants interacting. In extract 1, only one of the students and the moderator took an active part during the same period of time. This could be due to different factors: not having the sound tool ready in their computers, being too shy at the very beginning, or simply not knowing what to say. This situation changed by the end of the sessions. Thanks to direct contact with the CMC environment, all the participants improved their skills on IT and on the functioning of the whole project, so that their oral competence could be evaluated according to the criteria detailed in Table 1.

5.3 Qualitative analysis

Once the whole experiment had finished, a satisfaction survey was delivered to the participants. It was answered by 11 out of the 16 students who took part in the project. They were asked about the aspects of language they felt they had improved. The following figure shows the results:

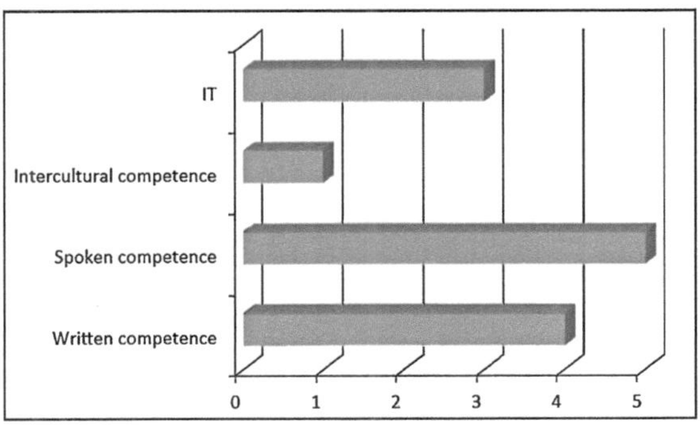

Fig. 6: Competence improvement

Most of them thought they had improved their spoken skills. It is important to see how many of them also believed that their level of written skills had improved as well, an element to take into account in a teaching context with a lack of communication in L2 like ours. It is remarkable that, although most of them maintained the same grades in the terms before and after the experiment, three of them increased their scores.

The initial intention of working in collaboration with students from other institutions in other parts of the world was unsuccessful due to several factors relating mainly to time. Nevertheless, UNED students were asked if this fact had decreased the quality of the whole project.

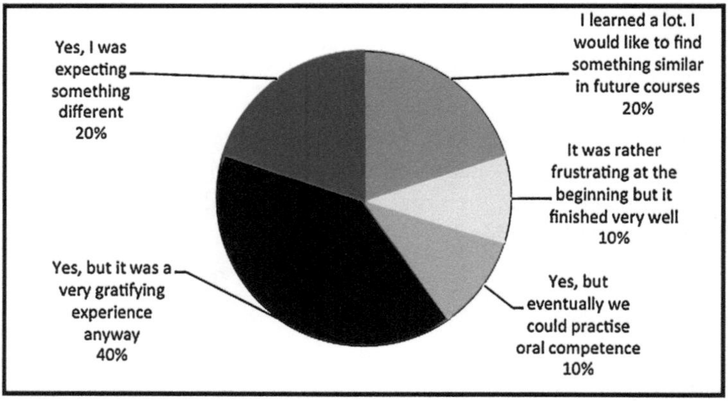

Fig. 7: *Levels of satisfaction*

As can be observed, just 20% of the respondents were disappointed with the final results.

Going through the marks obtained before and after the project, it can be observed how none of the participants achieved lower scores and some of them even improved considerably:

Table 3: *Marks*

Student	1st term	2nd term
1	*Aprobado*	*Aprobado*
2	*Suspenso*	*Aprobado*
3	*Aprobado*	*Aprobado*
4	*No presentado*	*No presentado*
5	*Aprobado*	*Notable*

6	*Notable*	*Notable*
7	*Notable*	*Notable*
8	*Notable*	*Notable*
9	*Aprobado*	*Notable*
10	*Aprobado*	*Notable*

Although not all of them submitted this survey, the table above clearly shows how, in general, the grades remained the same or increased. Finally, it would be important to bear in mind the amount of time devoted to the project by the participants:

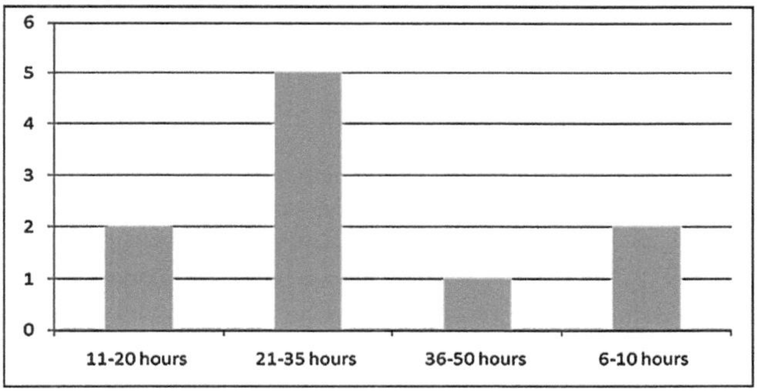

Fig. 8: *Time dedicated to the project*

Most of them devoted 21-35 hours in a period of six weeks. Taking into account the nature of these students and the lack of time they have to dedicate to studying, the effort was quite considerable.

6 Conclusions

This has been a rather ambitious project from the beginning, taking into account the limited time all its participants have to dedicate to any extra activity in their courses. Nevertheless, it has meant the beginning of many similar future experiences focused on the improvement of oral and intercultural competence of distance students. It has been very well accepted by all of them from its implementation as a new way of learning a foreign language at a distance and that is even more worthwhile than the results obtained. Perhaps these results could have been better if the teaching team had given more detailed instructions from the starting point, and if more time had been allocated for the students to get used to the new CMC tools in order to feel more confident earlier on. Nonetheless, this experience has been positive for most of the participants, as they have confirmed in the final presentations and the satisfaction survey.

Bibliography

Belz, J. A. (2003). Linguistic perspectives on the development of intercultural competence in telecollaboration. *Language Learning & Technology, 7*(2), 68-117. Retrieved from http://llt.msu.edu/vol7num2/belz/default.html (01/01/2013).

Berglund, T. (2009). Multimodal student interaction online: An ecological perspective. *ReCALL: The Journal of EUROCALL, 21*(2), 186-205.

Bower, M., & Hedberg, J. G. (2010). A quantitative multimodal discourse analysis of teaching and learning in a web-conferencing environment: The efficacy of student-centred learning designs. *Computers & Education, 54*(2), 462-478.

Boyle, R. (1995). Language teaching at a distance: From the first generation model to the third. *System, 23*(3), 283-294.

Breeze, R. (2003). Dimensions of intercultural education in the twenty-first century. *ESE: Estudios sobre Educación, 4*, 123-130. Retrieved from http://dialnet.unirioja.es/servlet/extart?codigo=650674 (01/01/2013).

Chiu, T., Liou, H., & Yeh, Y. (2007). A study of web-based oral activities enhanced by automatic speech recognition for EFL college learning. *Computer Assisted Language Learning, 20*(3), 209-233.

Ciekanski, M., & Chanier, T. (2008). Developing online multimodal verbal communication to enhance the writing process in an audio-graphic conferencing environment. *ReCALL: The Journal of EUROCALL, 20*(2), 162-182.

Council of Europe (2001). *Common European Framework of Reference for Languages: Learning, Teaching, Assessment*. Retrieved from http://www.coe.int/t/dg4/linguistic/ Source/Framework_EN.pdf (01/01/2013).

Egbert, J. L., & Petrie, G. M. (2005). *CALL Research Perspectives*. Mahwah, N.J.: L. Erlbaum Associates.

Enriquez, J. G. (2009). Discontent with content analysis of online transcripts. *ALT-J: Research in Learning Technology, 17*(2), 101-113).

Foster, P., & Tavakoli, P. (2009). Native speakers and task performance: Comparing effects on complexity, fluency, and lexical diversity. *Language Learning, 59*(4), 866-896.

Garrison, D. R. (1985). Three generations of technological innovations in distance education. *Distance Education, 6*(2), 235-241.

Hauck, M., & Youngs, B.L. (2008). Telecollaboration in multimodal environments: The impact on task design and learner interaction. *Computer Assisted Language Learning, 21*(2), 87-124.

Jaya, R. (2008). Skype voice chat: A tool for teaching oral communication. *Language in India, 8*(12), 9.

Jones, R.H. (2004). The problem of context in computer-mediated-communication. In E.L. Phillip, & R. Scollon (Eds.), *Discourse and Technology: Multimodal Discourse Analysis* (pp. 20-33). Washington, DC: Georgetown University Press.

Jung, U.O.H. (2005). CALL: Past, present and future, a bibliometric approach. *ReCALL: The Journal of EUROCALL, 17*(1), 4-17.

Kenning, M. (2010). Differences that make the difference: A study of functionalities in synchronous CMC. *ReCALL: The Journal of EUROCALL, 22*(1), 3-19.

Kessler, G. (2010). Fluency and anxiety in self-access speaking tasks: The influence of environment. *Computer Assisted Language Learning, 23*(4), 361-375.

Kress, G., & Leeuwen, T.V. (2001). *Multimodal Discourse*. London: Hodder Arnold Publication.

Lamy, M. N. (2004). Oral conversations online: Redefining oral competence in synchronous environments. *ReCALL, 16*(2), 520-538.

Liaw, M.-L., & Bunn-Le Master, S. (2010). Understanding telecollaboration through an analysis of intercultural discourse. *Computer Assisted Language Learning, 23*(1), 21-40).

Norris, S. (2004). *Analyzing Multimodal Interaction: A Methodological Framework*. New York: Routledge.

O'Dowd, R. (2007). Evaluating the outcomes of online intercultural exchange. *ELT Journal, 61*(2), 144-152).

O'Dowd, R., & Waire, P. (2009). Critical issues in telecollaborative task design. *Computer Assisted Language Learning, 22*(2), 173-188.

O'Rourke, B. (2008). The other C in CMC: What alternative data sources can tell us about text-based synchronous computer mediated communication and language learning. *Computer Assisted Language Learning, 21*(3), 227-251.

Raby, F. (2007). A triangular approach to motivation in computer assisted autonomous language learning (CAALL). *ReCALL: The Journal of EUROCALL, 19*(2), 181-201.

Ransdell, S. (2010). Online activity, motivation, and reasoning among adult learners. *Computers in Human Behavior, 26*(1), 70-73.

Rosell-Aguilar, F. (2005). Task design for audiographic conferencing: Promoting beginner oral interaction in distance language learning. *Computer Assisted Language Learning, 18*(5), 417-442.

Sauro, S. (2004). Cyberdiscursive tug-of-war: Learner repositioning in a multimodal CMC environment. *Working Papers in Educational Linguistics, 19*(2), 55-72.

Scarino, A. (2008). Community and culture in intercultural language learning. *Australian Review of Applied Linguistics, 31*(1), 5.1-5.15. Retrieved from http://www.nla.gov.au/openpublish/index.php/aral/article/viewFile/1976/2357 (01/01/2013).

Schwienhorst, K. (2004). Native-speaker/Non-native-speaker discourse in the MOO: Topic negotiation and initiation in a synchronous text-based environment. *Computer Assisted Language Learning, 17*(1), 35-50.

Thorpe, M. (1998). Assessment and 'third generation' distance education. *Distance Education, 19*(2), 265-287.

Tudini, V. (2005). Chatlines for beginners: Negotiating conversation at a distance. In B. Holmberg, M. Shelley, & C. White (Eds.), *Distance Education and Languages: Evalution and Change* (pp. 212-388). Clevedon, UK: Multilingual Matters.

Vinagre, M., & Muñoz, B. (2011). Computer-mediated corrective feedback and language accuracy in telecollaborative exchanges. *Language Learning & Technology*, *15*(1), 72-103. Retrieved from http://llt.msu.edu/issues/february2011/vinagremunoz.pdf (01/01/2013).

Wang, Y. (2006). Negotiation of meaning in desktop videoconferencing-supported distance language learning. *ReCALL*, *26*(1), 70-73.

Wang, Y., & Sun, C. (2001). Internet-based real time language education: Towards a fourth generation distance education. *CALICO Journal*, *18*(3), 539-561. Retrieved from https://calico.org/html/article_456.pdf (01/01/2013).

Yilmaz, Y., & Granena, G. (2010). The effects of task type in synchronous computer-mediated communication. *ReCALL*, *22*(1), 20-36.

Enhancing the Competency-based Approach to Learning in Literary Studies: Strategies and Resources

Miriam Borham-Puyal & Susana Olmos-Migueláñez

Abstract

In any degree, the reading of texts of a varied nature and extension is an essential activity; hence the interest in its appropriate planning and the need to achieve the development of autonomous learning strategies among university students in order to attain the reading efficiency and competence in critical analysis expected from them. Though these competencies are transversal to all subjects, it is obvious that their relevance is greater in Literary Studies.

Never losing sight of a competency-based approach and the need to enhance the use of autonomous learning strategies, this paper describes the design of resources and instruments aimed at the development and assessment of the abovementioned competencies. Implemented with software built into Moodle, these resources are varied (questionnaires, reading journals, etc.) and destined to help the students to efficiently read texts in English and to develop a critical approach to them so as to later produce their own discourse.

Among the conclusions, which are transferable to other subjects and degrees, we could highlight the enhancement of the students' reading comprehension and competence in critical analysis and the possibility of a learning-oriented assessment.

Introduction

Education is undoubtedly in the midst of a process of transformation and renewal, the competency-based approach to teaching having displaced the emphasis from the teacher and ex cathedra lecturing, to a student-centred teaching. In this sense, from a merely cognitive-oriented teaching-learning process, we have currently moved forward to an approach to it where skills, attitudes and values are as relevant as the contents themselves, if not more. This competency-based approach has profoundly affected the concept of literacy, which has now come to signify "the capacity of students to apply knowledge and skills in key subject areas and to analyse, reason and communicate effectively as they pose, solve and interpret problems in a variety of situations" (PISA Report, 2009: 13).

Within this general concept of literacy, in the present chapter we aim to highlight the idea of reading literacy. As the International Adult Literacy Survey (IALS) and the Programme for International Student Assessment (PISA) reports have respectively stated, reading is without question a cross-curricular competence and one of the cornerstones on which any area of knowledge lays its foundations. In any sphere or stage of the student's life or education, the reading of texts of a varied nature and extension is an essential activity; hence the interest in its appropriate planning (Salvador Mata *et al.*, 2007). Moreover, as we turn our attention to Higher Education, the need to achieve the development of autonomous learning strategies among university students in order to attain the reading efficiency expected from them (Cooper, 1984) becomes a crucial matter. Though reading is necessary in all degrees and subjects at university, it is obvious that its relevance is greater in those subjects which focus on the study of Literature. More specifically, in the new degrees in English Studies, oriented towards a competency-based approach, Literature subjects have as cornerstone this competence in reading, always understood as the relationship between reading fluency and comprehension (Gates, 1921; Taguchi *et al.*, 2006).[1]

However, this reading efficiency, focused on a literal or low-level understanding of the text, is not at the core of the competency-based notion of reading literacy. As has been stated in the relevant PISA report, "in reading, the capacity to develop interpretations of written material and to reflect on the content and qualities of text are central skills" (2009: 12). Taking the research conducted in the IALS even further, the PISA project describes reading literacy not only as the ability to understand a text, but also as the capacity to "use and reflect on a written text to achieve their [the students'] purposes", hence introducing an active element, for the students are asked to reflect on the text drawing on their own "thoughts and experiences" (2009: 14). If mere literal understanding is not enough for secondary-education students, it cannot be so for university ones. Higher-education students must be able to analytically and critically interpret what they read, no matter what degree or field they belong to. Furthermore, the need to develop this capacity moves beyond the stages of their primary, secondary or college education; reading literacy, conceived as the capacity to critically approach and comprehend the text, will be a fundamental part of their adult life and their professional career. Therefore, reading literacy should be highlighted in the curricula of all degrees, and very specifically in that of Literary Studies, in which subjects revolve around the capacity of their students to comprehend and critically interpret both primary and secondary sources, literary and scientific texts.

For the diagnosis, development and assessment of reading literacy, the design of specific resources and instruments is required. Though there have been some previous studies on the matter, these are still mostly limited to the phase of diagnosis. Among them, we could mention the creation of tests for the measurement of reading speed (Ronald, 2005), of reading speed and comprehension (Borham *et al.*, 2010), or the development of reading acceleration programmes

1 The relationship between reading speed and comprehension has been at the centre of an ongoing debate (see, for example, Broughton *et al.*, 1978; Champeau de López, 1993, 1996; Nuttall, 1982), and there is still some discussion on whether "they may be completely independent, or correlated, or cause and effect" (Bell, 2001).

(Champeau de López, 1993). Borham's study, developed among a group of teachers from the University of Salamanca, measured the speed (in number of words per minute) and the level of literal understanding of students from different degrees and nationalities who were studying Spanish and English at the Faculty of Philology. Multiple-choice questionnaires monitored their capacity to comprehend basic information contained in the text (details of the plot: names, locations, events) and allowed researchers to compare the different levels of understanding that arose among different groups of students or those readers facing texts in their L1 or L2. One of the most conspicuous advantages of this study was that it was conducted within the context of Spanish Higher Education, while prior research almost always took place abroad. An example would be Champeau's study with Higher Education students from Venezuela, which also focused on reading fluency. Champeau conducted a pre-test to measure the number of words per minute that her students could read, together with a questionnaire that aimed to ensure the students' comprehension. She designed a series of reading sessions, after which the test was taken again. Her results evidenced that there had been an increase in speed (from 120 to 170 words per minute), but not an improvement in comprehension, for the level of the latter had diminished in the post-test (from 78% to 67%).

These experiences can then only be seen as a first step, for they are not oriented towards the improvement of reading comprehension or of the capacity for critical analysis. Therefore, the creation of resources that could contribute to the enhancement of such determining competencies for all Higher Education students, and more so for those who have to face Literary Studies, seemed absolutely necessary. In this respect, the work developed by a research group of the University of Barcelona could be particularly useful. This group of teachers has created material to use in Literature subjects which aims to enhance both the reading comprehension and the later critical production, combining PowerPoint presentations to introduce the topic, questionnaires on the reading and guided questions to be answered in a written essay during or after the reading.[2]

Despite their usefulness, there is one fundamental element which all the aforementioned experiences have not taken into account. The new organization in

2 Grup d'Innovació Docent [Innovative Teaching Group] "Estratègies per al desenvolupament de les habilitats de lectura i escriptura de l'alumnat de literatura de Filologia Anglesa" [Strategies for Developing Reading and Writing Skills in English Philology Students of Literature] (Code: 2004bGID-UB/09), coordinated by Enric Monforte, which later became "INDIGO: Estudis de narrativa en llengua anglesa" [INDIGO: Studies of Fiction in English] (Code: 2009GID-UB/04), coordinated by Ana Moya. The abovementioned resources are available at http://diposit.ub.edu/dspace/handle/2445/13522 (01/01/2013).

competencies and the exponential technological advance in all areas of Higher Education (teaching, research, and administration) and, more specifically, their repercussion on the possible enhancement of the conception of new teaching-learning methodologies (Colás, 2005), have rendered indispensable a self-critical approach to the traditional resources and instruments employed in the classroom for the development and assessment of the students' reading comprehension and capacity for critical analysis. When teaching at university is structured around competencies, the organizational changes do not exclusively affect our teaching methodology, but also have an impact on the learning processes and on assessment. Especially important is the change in the latter; in an education oriented towards a competency-based approach, we must highlight the idea of a formative assessment rather than a summative one (Robinson & Udall, 2006), stressing the improvement of the students' learning, as we facilitate and/or promote a thoughtful attitude. Formative assessment is defined as "assessment that is specifically intended to provide feedback on performance to improve and accelerate learning" (Sadler, 1998: 77). In this sense, as Nicol & Milligan have stated, formative assessment and feedback can be used in contexts in which face-to-face and online learning are integrated –as is the case in this study– in order to promote the development of self-regulated learning (SRL) (2006: 64), which is one of the aims of the competency-based approach to learning. These authors subsequently analyse the role that technology-supported assessment could have for the good practice of such an essential aspect as is feedback in a competency-based teaching-learning process.[3]

The use of ICT's for the improvement and assessment of learning most definitely opens new fields and allows the development of innovative techniques and, with them, numerous advantages for the execution of a task such as assessment, which, although indispensable, is highly laborious for teachers (Olmos, 2008). The most important of those advantages would be the possibility to provide immediate results and a detailed analysis of them, as well as constant and even more immediate feedback to correct mistakes or to further the students'

3 Nicol & Milligan work on the basis of the thorough description of good feedback practice provided by Nicol & Macfarlane-Dick (2004). These authors assert that good feedback practice "helps clarify what good performance is (goals, criteria, expected standards); facilitates the development of reflection and self-assessment in learning; delivers high-quality information to students about their learning; encourages teacher and peer dialogue around learning; encourages positive motivational beliefs and self-esteem; provides opportunities to close the gap between current and desired performance; provides information to teachers that can be used to help shape the teaching" (Nicol & Millligan, 2006: 64-65). This idea of what feedback should allow is shared by the authors of the present article, and has guided much of the reflection and work done.

reflection. ICT's also allow a more efficient teaching-learning process, an easier adaptation to the students, the improvement of the development of skills related to technologies –another cross-curricular competence–, the chance to repeat an exam several times, the inclusion of multimedia elements in the assessment, or the assessment of a wide range of topics, among other advantages (Olmos, 2008).

Taking all these facts into account, the use of new technologies, and, more specifically, of virtual platforms which allow the possibility of e-assessment, such as Moodle, seemed ideal not only to enhance the autonomy and reflection of the students within their own learning process, but also to help teachers in overcrowded classes where the European Framework must be implemented without increasing the cost or, in many cases, without even having more material resources available. We will subsequently describe what strategies were used and what resources and instruments were created in order to motivate students and to improve the reading comprehension and the competence in critical analysis in an online environment, and how those resources were used or could be used within a classroom.

Method

The need to reassess the role of reading comprehension and the capacity for critical analysis in the new degrees in English Studies, as well as the traditional strategies, resources or instruments for their assessment, was acknowledged by a group of teachers from the English Department at the University of Salamanca who were involved in an innovation project oriented towards the improvement of online English Literature and Culture courses.[4]

This body of teachers together reflected on the adaptation of their respective subjects to the European Framework and to the pressing need to introduce ICTs in Spanish Higher Education. Having decided that the objectives had to be conceived in terms of competencies, in this case, the competence in reading comprehension and in critical analysis, the question of how to develop and assess these competencies became the cornerstone of the present case study. These teachers then collaborated with others from the University Institute of Education Science (IUCE), and attended several courses on the use of Moodle (Studium-USAL), by means of which the creation process of resources and instruments to

4 Teaching Innovation Project granted by the University of Salamanca: "Diseño de recursos y módulos interactivos en el campus virtual para las materias de Literatura y Cultura en el Grado y Posgrado de Estudios Ingleses". ID10/083. Coordinators: Pedro Javier Pardo García and Miriam Borham Puyal.

develop and assess the abovementioned competencies could take place in an online learning environment.

Though always in consensus, the resources and instruments were later designed independently by each of these teachers to be implemented in their respective online courses. However, owing to the great number of students enrolled in the different classes –between 100 and 180–, the implementation took place first in two Master's' subjects, *The Rise of the Novel* and *Metafiction in Literature and Film,* with three and five students respectively, in which it was easier to monitor the use of these resources and instruments and the response of the students towards them. Therefore, the early stage of this study was conducted in these two courses, and the results we introduce are presently limited to them.[5]

From the range of resources that the platforms provided, this body of teachers agreed that questionnaires, reading journals, databases, glossaries, wikis and written assignments would be suitable in order to develop and assess the students' reading comprehension and critical analysis. All of these resources were hence elaborated within the framework of the aforementioned subjects. Taking one of the readings in the syllabus as starting point –in this particular case, the novel *The Life and Opinions of Tristram Shandy, Gentleman* by Laurence Sterne–, a questionnaire of 25 multiple-choice items was created, covering characters and events throughout the novel. Multiple-choice questions were preferred over those which involved a short answer, for they provided an unequivocal answer which the latter do not. That is, in those questions to be answered with a short phrase or sentence, any deviation from the wording chosen by the teacher would incur in an error. Though the teacher could choose variables (for example: Tristram, Tristram Shandy, Shandy), there would always be the risk of a misspelling or of a possibility the teacher had not contemplated, which would alter the result. As for the questions which demanded a short essay, it would not be possible to systematize the assessment in the same way as with multiple-choice questions.

After its completion, this questionnaire was uploaded for the students to answer. In this particular case, as we were working with Master's students whose literal understanding was in a certain measure taken for granted, it was considered voluntary work to motivate a closer reading of the text and to be used for

---

5 The authors are extremely thankful to Prof. Pedro Javier Pardo García for so willingly agreeing to collaborate in the present study, for so thoroughly and relevantly designing and implementing most of these resources and for allowing the use of his classes and his students for the present case study. Only his usual self-effacement has prevented his name from being written together with that of the other authors.

the self-assessment of their reading comprehension. Each student then completed it individually and outside the classroom.

In order to work on particular words, concepts or works, the students were also asked to create a glossary in which to define relevant terms related to the course's syllabus. Each student contributed to it by providing thoughtful definitions of several key theoretical concepts which belonged both to the primary and secondary sources and which were to be referred to in class. These definitions could be supported with bibliography or quotations, being able to provide external links or even to create hyperlinks to other contents from the online course. Together with the glossary, students also participated in the creation of a cooperative film database in which they had to develop entries for a novel and three films in which any of the kinds of metafiction explained in class could be observed and which they were later to discuss in a final interview with the teacher. In these entries, they had to include some compulsory information determined by the teacher, who in this case elected the following fields: title, credits, posters, storyline, keywords, review and selected links.

Another resource aimed at the creation of a critical perception of the texts and the development of a personal discourse was the reading journal. Each student elaborated their own online journal. Students were able to edit it throughout the course, adding or deleting information, providing their opinion on one particular work of fiction or aspect of that same work, or even a comparative analysis of two or more readings within the list provided in the syllabus. There was no assigned time, the students could write their journals as they read the texts, each at his or her own pace. The teacher read the journals and also edited his feedback, sometimes providing suggestions for further reading or for matters relevant to the text that could be of interest to the student for his or her better comprehension of it. The student could then choose to incorporate the teacher's suggestions and hence edit his or her entry.

Together with these resources, in this particular online campus, teachers also have at their disposal other options, such as the submission of written assignments. Working on previous works which state the value of essay assignments as a way of both assessing (Prosser & Webb, 1994) and promoting deep approaches to learning (Scouller, 1998), and on the importance of the students' understanding of the assessment criteria involved in essay writing (Harrington *et al.*, 2006; Merry *et al.*, 1998), these essays were based on a set of questions on the reading which covered methodological or conceptual matters discussed in the course and which guided their comprehension of the novels in the syllabus. The assessment criteria had been discussed with the students before any submission took place. Three essays in total were requested, all with a different approach to the reading. The students wrote their individual papers and uploaded them. The essays were then graded online and, more importantly, personal feedback was provided: the teacher offered suggestions, positive reinforcements, etc., without having to wait to be in class. In this particular case, the teacher provided the assessment and the feedback; however, as has been asserted before, Moodle allows other ways of assessment: hetero-assessment, co-assessment or self-assessment. The platform also provides the possibility of single or multiple uploads, as well as of re-submissions. The option to set a deadline for the submissions is also granted, together with the acceptance or refusal of late texts. Teachers in this class agreed on a deadline of one week for each paper and the rejection of late submissions.

Finally, students were asked to collaboratively create a wiki on the topic of narratology, an essential term in critical theory and the study of literature. This wiki had to include several essential terms which had proved problematic for students in previous years. Ideally, the wiki had to develop as an organic text, with participation from all students, who had to read their peers' contribution and then edit the text, adding or deleting information. The teacher monitored via the platform the involvement of the different students, as well as their input, and feedback from both teacher and peers was provided.

All these resources not only aimed at the development of the abovementioned competencies, but were also designed to be complemented by the use of instruments through which to conduct both a summative and formative assessment of the students' performance. These instruments answered to pre-established criteria which were made known to the students in advance. In the framework of these two subjects, the criteria by which to assess the students' performances, products or activities could be divided into three groups: formal, attitudinal and conceptual. Formal criteria would include such aspects as the grammatical correctness, the lexical accuracy, the coherence or the presentation of the students' written products. Attitudinal criteria would serve to assess the students' participation in the discussion conducted in class or the different forums; their contribution to any form of team-work; their autonomy in the use of primary and secondary sources; or even their observance of the established deadlines. Finally, and more relevantly for this study, criteria related to conceptual values were utilised, namely, the reference to primary and secondary sources, whether those provided by the teacher or those researched by the student; the identification and exposition of facts and abstract ideas found in the text; the relevance of the production in relation to the task proposed, for instance, if they answered the questions on the text put forward by the teacher; and, ultimately, the creation of a personal and coherent discourse on the reading. All these would be especially important to assess the students' competence in critical analysis.

Lastly, among the several assessment instruments that could be employed, the following were developed: checklists to assess what tasks were done; rating or grading scales to assess the performance and the resulting product; and the analysis of the assignments.

Results

The most evident result was the creation of the abovementioned resources, as well as of the assessment instruments. We subsequently provide examples of the resources created:

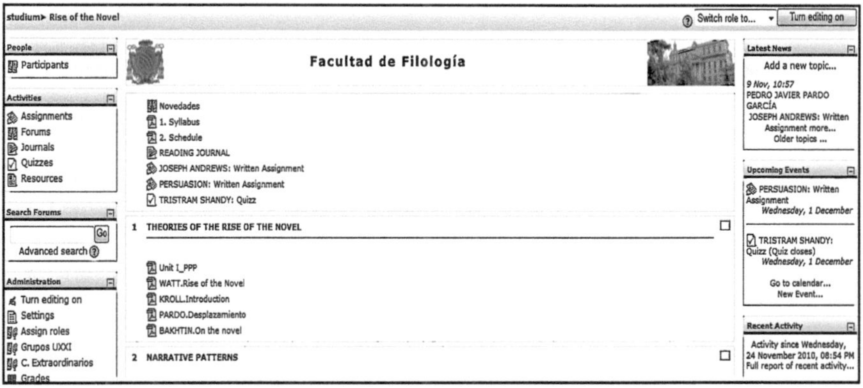

Fig. 1: Studium-USAL

Studium is extremely user-friendly and its interface allows employing it in a very intuitive manner. The resources were integrated within the online subjects in Studium, being easily located and used by the students.

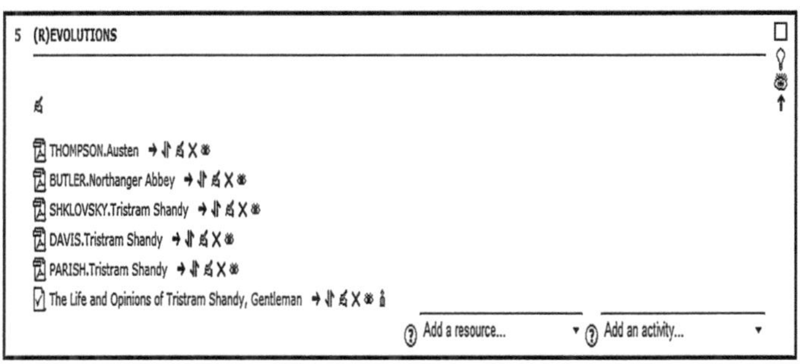

Fig. 2: Resources and questionnaire

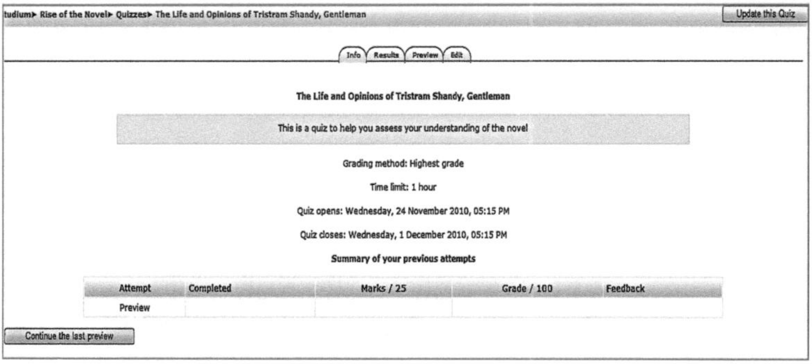

Fig. 3: *Questionnaire*

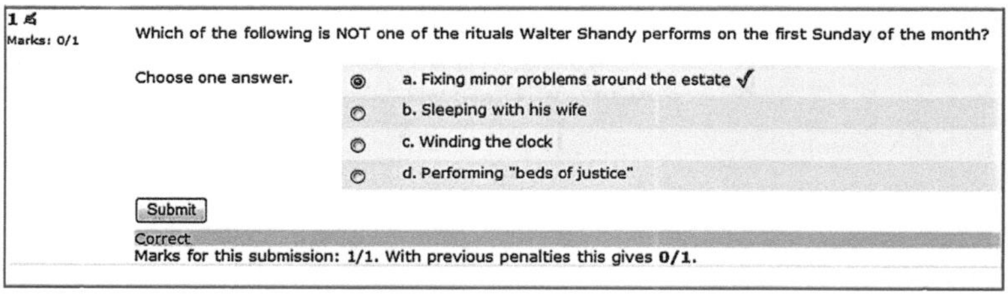

Fig. 4: *Questionnaire*

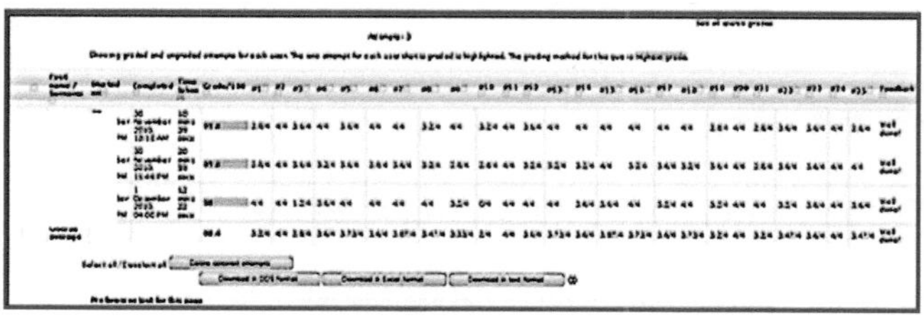

Fig. 5: *Results of the questionnaire*

In the same way as the *multiple-choice questionnaire* employed by Borham *et al.* in previous years (2010), this online questionnaire evidenced the *literal* understanding of the text, which in these students proved to be very high. Of course, this questionnaire could be repeated and provided immediate feedback on the right or wrong answers, something which the printed versions employed in the abovementioned case did not do.

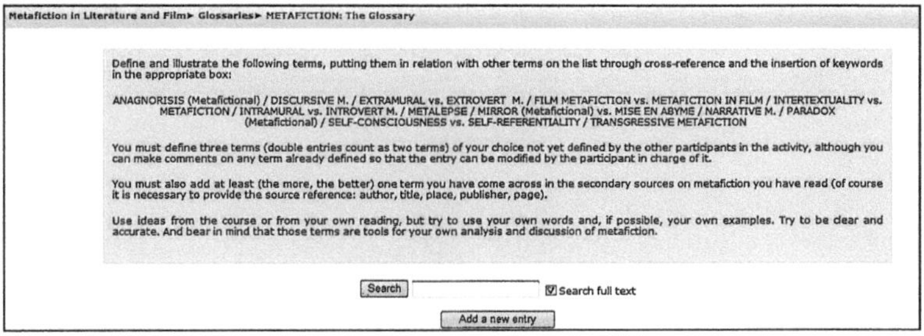

Fig. 6: *Glossary*

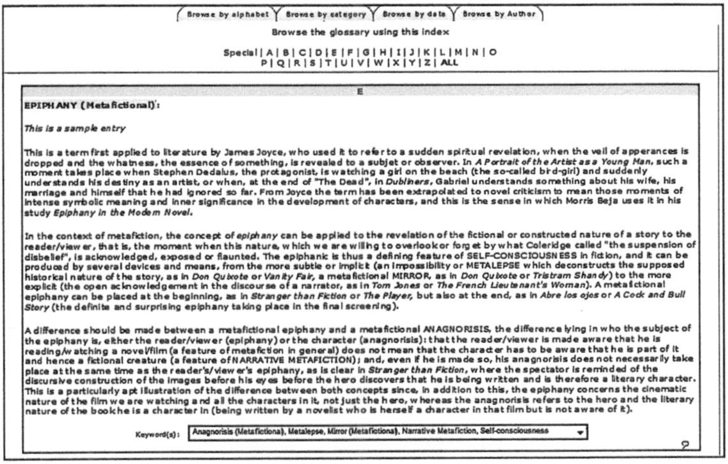

Fig. 7: *Glossary entry*

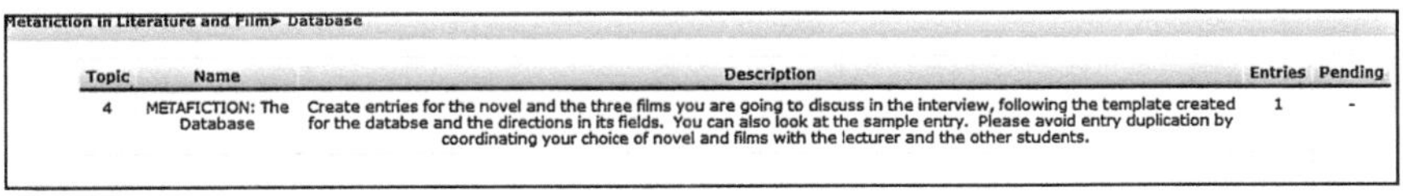

Fig. 8: *Database*

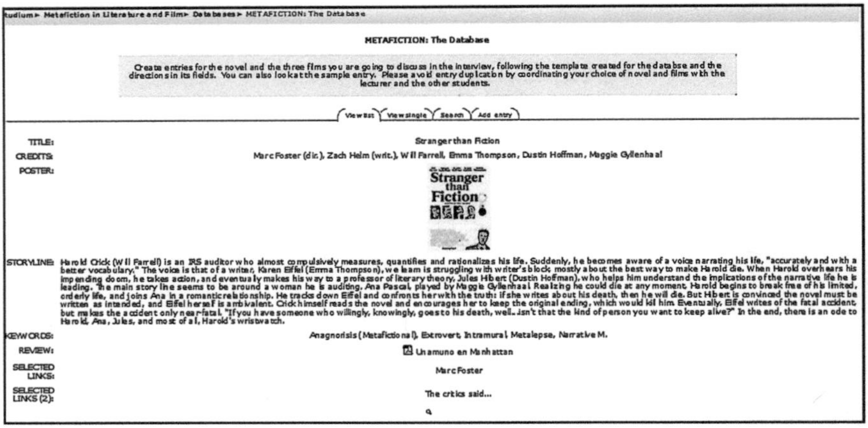

Fig. 9: *Database*

Glossaries focused on terms that could help students acquire a better understanding of the texts and the subject as a whole. It was then not only a matter of understanding the meaning of isolated words or concepts, but of working and reflecting on them in relation to the different texts referred to in class, in order to lead to a later critical analysis of their content. The same could be said of *databases,* which evidenced the internalization of the concepts of metafiction by having to apply them to the identification and analysis of those films that displayed metafictional traits. In addition to these facts, both glossaries and databases permit the incorporation of pictures, attachments, links to web pages, hyperlinks to other elements of the platform, etc.; thereby, they are highly interactive and motivate the students' involvement in the search for material and in the use of the opportunities whihc new technologies provide, once again enhancing such a cross-curricular competence as the use of ICTs. Moreover, they provide the possibility for different forms of assessment, such as self-assessment or co-assessment, which involve the student in his or her own process of learning, as well as in that of his or her peers.

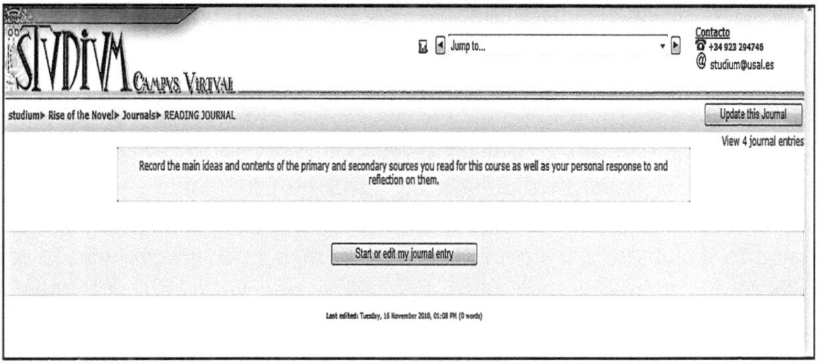

Fig. 10: *Reading Journal*

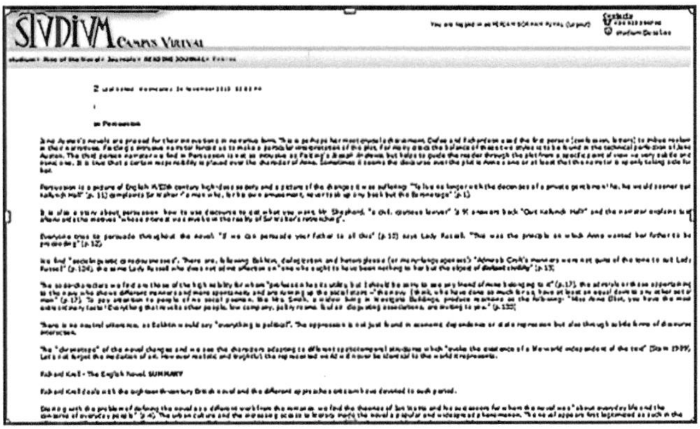

Fig. 11: *Reading Journal*

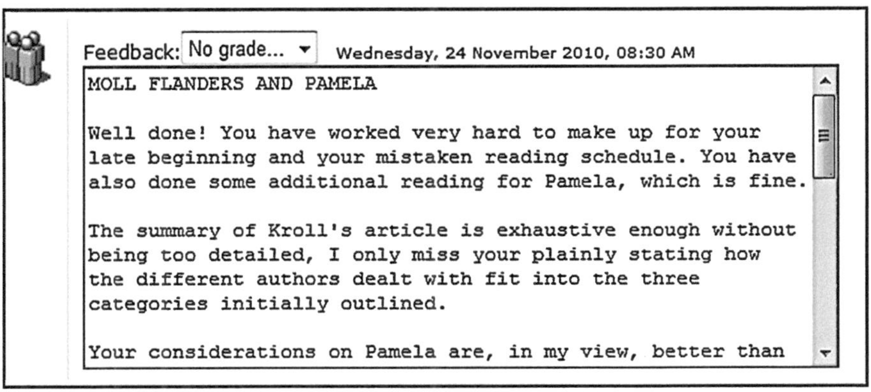

Fig. 12: *Reading Journal*

The use of *reading journals* allowed the teacher to verify if the students had achieved a *deeper* understanding of the text; that is, if they could understand the more complex ideas in the novel rather than just easy facts or events. One of the most important advantages was, as we can see in the figure above, that the teacher could provide constant feedback on the student's performance. Hence, teachers and students established a dialogue that helped the latter's comprehension and production of a critical discourse. In that sense, the use of reading journals promoted in the students the need to reflect on their own comprehension of the texts, therefore improving their capacity to create *internal* feedback to their own production, together with their competence in critical analysis in relation to the work they had read.

In conclusion, between the questionnaire, the database, the glossary and the reading journal, both the *literal* and the *critical* levels of understanding could be developed and assessed, hence complementing each other.

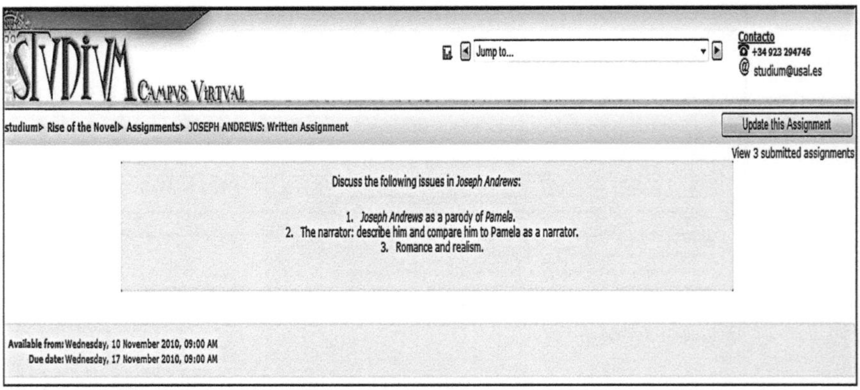

Fig. 13: Written assignment

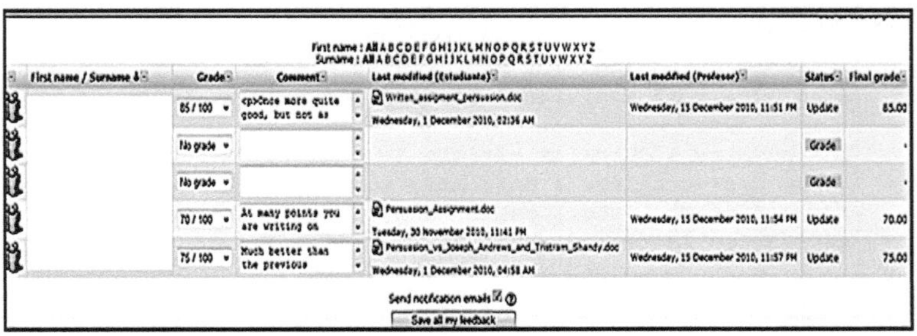

Fig. 14: Grades and remarks for written assignments

As has been previously stated, one of the most relevant objectives in literary studies is for the students to be capable of *producing* a personal and critical discourse. The journal is the first step towards this kind of production on the students' behalf. However, it usually lacks the structure or the thought of more formal pieces of writing. The *writing of guided texts* then proves a useful resource to delve deeper into the students' capacity to create a coherent critical discourse, both in form and in content. The essays in which students have to answer reflectively and analytically to questions on the reading not only enhance their competence in critical analysis, but also provide an opportunity for a greater implication of the students in their own learning: students become autonomous in their search for and use of the primary and secondary sources to be quoted in their written works; they will have to be rigorous in their analysis and their adaptation to the demanded format or content, as well as become responsible for their own writing process, as they will have to respect the deadlines. Obviously, this is not a new task in the field of teaching or, more particularly, in that of assessment; however, the possibility of managing it in an online environment enhances the immediacy of the feedback and facilitates the upload of more than one text, or the re-submission of a particular essay.

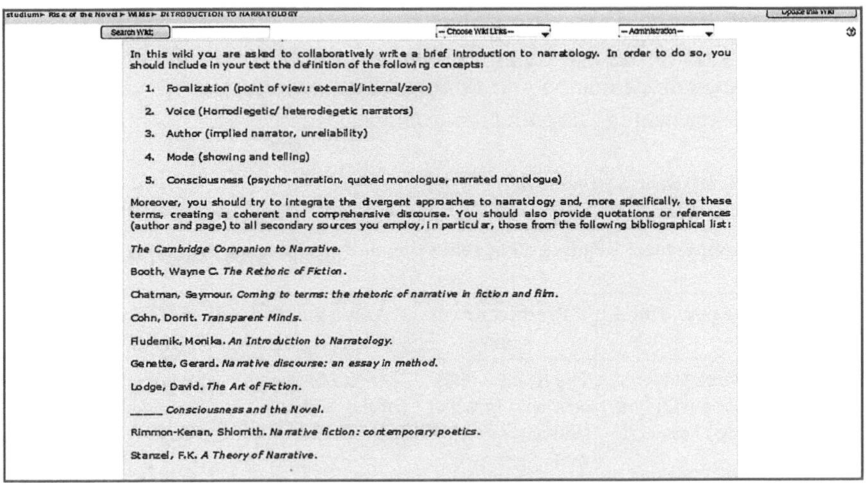

Fig. 15: *Wiki*

If written assignments afford the chance for students to individually develop their critical approach to reading, the *wiki* provides the context in which students can co-operate in order to reach a collaborative analysis and comprehension of a particular work under examination or, as in this case, of a whole body of critical writing. Once again, it offers the opportunity for feedback from both the teacher and, more importantly, the student's peers, for the writing develops in an organic way, by means of the continuous readings, suggestions and production of all the team members. It also enhances internal feedback, as it demands re-reading and rewritings from the student in order to create the final coherent critical discourse. The fact that the teacher can monitor who contributes, as well as what and how the different students share, ensures the participation of the whole group, hence avoiding the frustration of the students in the cases where the collaboration is being unequal. In larger classes, such as those in which these resources and instruments will be subsequently implemented, the possibility of students working in groups could prove highly rewarding, as we count on the experience of other teachers in different subjects.

As for the assessment instruments employed to estimate the students' performance and products, we now offer an example of one of them. In the first table there is an instance of assessment systematizing, in which what is to be assessed and how to do so are clearly stated, while the second one provides an example of a rating scale in which the aforementioned criteria are included, leading to an overall estimation and final grading of the students' wiki, the task subject to assessment in this particular example.

Table 1: Assessment systematizing

Assessed competence: Reading comprehension and competence in critical analysis			
Task to be performed	**Product or resource**	**Assessment strategy**	**Rating scale**
Groups of three students should create a wiki with the following characteristics: 1. Topic: narratology 2. Structure: - Definition - Discussion 3. Use of secondary sources.	The result would be a wiki in which students would write their own introduction to narratology	Direct observation of the students' performance Analysis of the task Hetero-assessment Self-assessment Co-assessment	Criteria Grading criteria

Table 2: Rating scale

Rating scale					
Dimensions	1 Not adequate	2 Slightly adequate	3 Sufficiently adequate	4 Very adequate	5 Completely adequate
Presentation					
1. Observance of the layout					
2. Coherence					
3. Grammatical correctness					
4. Lexical accuracy					
Attitude					
5. Observance of the deadline					
6. Level of implication and participation					
Content					
7. Observance of the proposed topic					
8. Relevant content					
9. Use of relevant bibliography					
10. Originality					
11. Creation of a personal and critical discourse					
Overall estimation					
Grading	% Hetero-assessment: 80% Co-assessment: 15% Self-assessment: 5%				

Discussion

The competency-based approach and the use of ICTs in the classroom have changed the way in which students and teachers face the teaching-learning process and have made the development of new teaching and assessing strategies, resources and instruments undeniably necessary. The creation of the abovementioned resources on virtual platforms, such as Moodle, has proved to allow a better adjustment to the student and to his or her needs, especially within the frame of the Bologna Process and the European Higher Education Area. These online resources contribute to enhance the student's autonomous or self-regulated learning, while they also improve his or her use of new technologies. Moreover, an online learning environment, and the employment of Moodle in particular, also has countless advantages in relation to the assessment of competencies such as reading comprehension and the competence in critical analysis; to the possibility of self-assessment, co-assessment, hetero-assessment and pair-assessment processes; or to the repetition of tests as many times as necessary. More importantly, it provides the chance for the constant, and sometimes even immediate, feedback from the teacher, from the student's own classmates or from the students themselves, hence fulfilling the objective of aiming towards a formative assessment which complements the traditional summative one.

In conclusion, the use of these online resources, together with assessment instruments which can also be implemented online, though still in an early stage, favours the development of the students' reading comprehension and competence in critical analysis, as well as a criterial, systematic and comprehensive assessment of these same competencies.

Biliography

Bell, T. (2001). Extensive reading: Speed and comprehension. *The Reading Matrix, 1*(1). Retrieved from http://www.readingmatrix.com/articles/bell/article.pdf (01/01/2013).

Borham-Puyal, M. *et al.* (2010). Lectura extensiva en inglés en la planificación con ECTS: ¿A qué velocidad lee un estudiante de filología inglesa? In L. Pérez Ruiz, I. Parrado Román, & P. Tabarés Pérez (Eds.), *Estudios de metodología de la lengua inglesa [V]* (pp. 433-440). Valladolid: Secretariado de Publicaciones, Universidad de Valladolid.

Broughton, G., Brumfit, C., Flavell, R., Hill, P., & Pincas, A. (1978). *Teaching English as a Foreign Language*. London: Routledge & Kegan Paul.

Champeau de López, C. (1993). Developing reading speed. *English Teaching Forum 31*(1), 50-51.

Champeau de López, C. (1996). Increasing reading speed in English as a foreign language. *Bulletin of Language Science and Humanities 10*, 183-203.

Colás, P. (2005). La formación universitaria en base a competencias. In P. Colás, & J. de Pablos (Coords.), *La universidad en la Unión Europea. El Espacio Europeo de Educación Superior y su impacto en la docencia* (pp. 101-123). Málaga: Aljibe.

Cooper, M. (1984). Linguistic competence of practiced and unpracticed non-native readers of English. In J. C. Alderson, & A. H. Urquhart, *Reading in a Foreign Language* (pp. 122-135). London: Longman.

Gates, A. I. (1921). An experimental and statistical study of reading and reading tests. *The Journal of Educational Psychology, 12*(6), 303-314.

Harrington, K. *et al.* (2006). Using core assessment criteria to improve essay writing. In C. Bryan, & K. Clogg (Eds.), *Innovative Assessment in Higher Education* (pp. 110-119). London/New York: Routledge.

Merry, S., Orsmond, P., & Reiling, K. (1998). Biology students' and tutors' understandings of 'a good essay'. In C. Rust (Ed.), *Improving Student Learning: Improving Students as Learners* (pp. 202-205). Oxford: Oxford Centre for Staff and Learning Development.

Nicol, D. J., & Milligan, C. (2006). Rethinking technology-supported assessment practices in relation to seven principles of good feedback practice. In C. Bryan, & K. Clogg (Eds.), *Innovative Assessment in Higher Education* (pp. 64-77). London/New York: Routledge.

Nicol, D. J., & Macfarlane-Dick, D. (2004). Rethinking formative assessment in HE: A theoretical model and seven principles of good feedback practice. *Higher Education Academy*. Retrieved from http://www.enhancementthemes.ac.uk/documents/events/20040604/NicolMacfarlane-Dickpaper-revised.pdf (01/01/2013).

Nuttall, C. (1982). *Teaching Reading Skills in a Foreign Language.* London: Heinemann Educational.

Olmos, S. (2008). *Evaluación formativa y sumativa de estudiantes universitarios: Aplicación de las tecnologías a la evaluación educativa.* Salamanca: Ediciones Universidad de Salamanca, Colección Vítor, 228.

PISA Report (2009). *Assessment Framework. Key Competencies in Reading, Mathematics and Science.* Retrieved from http://www.oecd.org/dataoecd/11/40/44455820.pdf (01/01/2013).

Prosser, M., & Webb, C. (1994). Relating the process of undergraduate essay writing to the finished product. *Studies in Higher Education, 19*, 125-138.

Robinson, A., & Udall, M. (2006). Using formative assessment to improve student learning through critical reflection. In C. Bryan, & K. Clegg (Eds.), *Innovative Assessment in Higher Education* (pp. 92-99). London/New York: Routledge.

Ronald, S. (2005). *The Scientific Foundations for RocketReader.* Retrieved from http://www.rocketreader.com/research/rocketreader_whitepaper.pdf (01/01/2013).

Sadler, D. R. (1998). Formative assessment: Revisiting the territory. *Assessment in Education, 5*(1), 77-84.

Salvador Mata, F., Gallego, J. L., & Mieres, C. G. (2007). Habilidades lingüísticas y comprensión lectora. Una investigación empírica. *Bordón 59*(1), 153-166.

Scouller, K. (1998). The influence of assessment method on students' learning approaches: Multiple choice question examination versus assignment essay. *Higher Education, 35*, 453-472.

Taguchi, E., Gorsuch, G., & Sasamoto, E. (2006). Developing second and foreign language reading fluency and its effect on comprehension: A missing link. *The Reading Matrix 6*(2), 1-18.

Competency Development and Evaluation: Student-centred Assessment Methodologies Related to the EHEA

Kent Löfgren

Abstract

This paper concerns university teachers' evaluations of their students' competences (knowledge and skills) and discusses student-centred and competency-based higher education in the European Higher Education Area (EHEA). The argument is that a dramatic shift of focus has taken place in European higher education, from teacher-centred to student-centred education, and teachers in this system need to familiarize themselves with this shift and the related concepts. For example, the curricula and assessment methodologies in today's universities emphasize competences and focus on what students can perform and how these competences can be related to work. In order to acquire a comprehensive understanding, knowledge about the historical roots behind student-centred education and competency development may be required, and this paper attempts to provide some of this information. With these new insights, a choice will need to be made: should these trends be resisted and the old methods of providing courses be adhered to, or should the winds of change be accepted and adaptations be made –or perhaps the best choice lies somewhere in between these two options? Regardless of one's emotions, such a personal choice should be based upon and motivated by the best information available.

The Bologna Process and the EHEA

The European Higher Education Area (EHEA) is an international project in Europe and beyond, in which higher education systems are made more transparent and in sync with one another. Founded in 2010 as a result of the Bologna Declaration (1999), it currently comprises 47 national states and a number of consultative organizational members. The historical roots of the Bologna Process can be traced back to a number of earlier agreements; it is important to pay attention to these in order to fully understand the processes and the EHEA of today.

The 1997 Lisbon Recognition Convention and the 1998 Sorbonne Declaration

The Lisbon Recognition Convention is an agreement between a number of member states of the Council of Europe and a number of important states in the field of higher education, including, for example, Australia, Canada, New Zealand and the USA. The Convention stipulates that degrees and periods of study must be recognised "unless a substantial difference can be shown" (Lisbon Recognition Convention, 1997: 7) by the institution that is charged with recognition. The Sorbonne Declaration, signed in 1998 by four European countries (France, Germany, Italy and the United Kingdom), was an agreement regarding higher education with the purpose of coming to a common understanding and working together to encourage study periods abroad, to improve excellence in study and research, to develop a common understanding of teaching and learning and to encourage cooperation. In order to enable comparison, the Sorbonne Declaration put forward a system of cycles and a system of credits (the European Credit Transfer System, ECTS). The Declaration ends with a call to other states "to join us in this objective and [...] [to] all European Universities to consolidate Europe's standing in the world through continuously improved and updated education for its citizens" (Sorbonne Declaration, 1998: 3).

The 1999 Bologna Declaration and the ECTS system

The 29 countries that signed the Bologna Declaration in 1999 agreed to support the ideas expressed in the Sorbonne Declaration and to co-ordinate policies in order to reach a number of objectives, particularly to "establish the European area of higher education and to promote the European system of higher education world-wide" (Bologna Declaration, 1999: 3). Among the main stakeholders in the Bologna Process –a process implemented from 1999 through 2010– were the European University Association, the European Association of Institutions of Higher Education, the European Association for Quality Assurance in Higher Education, the Council of Europe, the European Commission, UNESCO, the European Students' Union, and the various government ministers responsible for higher education (Heinze & Knill, 2008). The stakeholders held a number of biannual meetings in Paris (1999), Prague (2001), Berlin (2003), Bergen (2005), London (2007), and Leuven and Louvain-la-Neuve (2009).

The Bologna Declaration is not a legally binding document; instead, it is an agreement in which the participating countries voluntarily synchronize their systems of higher education based on ideas previously expressed in the Sorbonne Declaration (1998). This synchronization implies that students' qualifications are defined in terms of learning outcomes, rather than in terms of the length of study, which, in turn, means that the basic unit has shifted from the number of professor contact hours to student workload. It also requires the adoption of determined levels of higher education qualifications; for example, the bachelor's and master's degrees.

The European Credit Transfer System (ECTS), which was discussed in both the Sorbonne and the Bologna declarations, is based on the workload required by the average student to achieve the objectives of a course; that is to say, to successfully complete the work required and pass the obligatory examinations, which in turn are based on the course's syllabi and expected learning outcomes. The ECTS is an instrument implemented to recognize students' study-periods, but it is important to remember that the purpose of the original Declarations, including the introduction of the ECTS system, was not simply to assist students. Another –equally important– purpose was to sharpen Europe's competitiveness, as Adam (2001) reminds us. The politicians and policy makers did not draft the Sorbonne and Bologna declarations based on unselfish philanthropy; rather, they were concerned "about the nature and competitiveness of European higher education" (Adam, 2001: 292).

Student-centred education and learning outcomes

The terms student-centred education and learning outcomes (NCIHE, 1997; Otter, 1993) are given prominent places in the Bologna Process and in the documents released by the higher education ministers. The Leuven/Louvain-la-Neuve Communiqué from 2009, for example, discusses the importance of student-centred learning; in it, the ministers stipulate that student-centred learning "requires empowering individual learners" and "new approaches to teaching and learning", as well as "effective support and guidance structures and a curriculum focused more clearly on the learner" (Leuven/Louvain-la-Neuve Communiqué, 2009: 3). Student-centred education includes the possibility for students to choose their own study paths during their years at higher education institutions and departments. The ministers acknowledge this and conclude that the curricular reform taking place in the EHEA will "be an ongoing process leading to high quality, flexible and more individually tailored education paths" (Leuven/Louvain-la-Neuve Communiqué, 2009: 3). From reading the Communiqué, it is clear that the ministers are confident that student-centred learning should be the goal of curricular reforms during the Bologna Process. The term learning outcomes is also prominently discussed in the ministerial communiqués, such as the Berlin Communiqué from 2003.

Competency-based education

The concept of competences has been used in various educational settings over the last decades, both in the USA and in Europe. In the context of the Bologna Process, the term was used in the Bologna Declaration, which stated that "a Europe of knowledge" was an important factor for growth and for providing Europe's citizens with "the necessary competences to face the challenges of the new millennium," (Bologna Declaration, 1999: 1). The concept was also extensively used in the Tuning Educational Structures in Europe project. The aim of the Tuning project, which began in 2001, was to tune the educational structures in European higher education and to invite debate regarding subject-specific and general competences (Tuning, 2006). At the Prague Ministerial meeting in 2001, it was stated that Europe's citizens should be able to "effectively use their qualifications, competencies and skills" throughout the EHEA (Prague Communiqué, 2001: 1). It is interesting to notice that the Prague Communiqué uses the term "competencies", instead of "competences", unlike other communiqués– it is not clear if this was a conscious decision from the ministers.

Four years after the Bologna Declaration, the concept of competences was also discussed in the Graz Declaration (2003), published by the European University Association (EUA), where the continued development of a common definition of competences was emphasised. Later the same year, when the ministers responsible for higher education met in Berlin, they acknowledged the argument put forward in the Graz Convention (Berlin Communiqué, 2003). Thus, the Berlin Communiqué states that the member states should "elaborate a framework of comparable and compatible qualifications" (Berlin Communiqué, 2003: 4) and that this framework should describe qualifications in terms of learning outcomes and competences. In the same communiqué, the ministers also declared the need to reaffirm the Lisbon Recognition Convention and to enhance the competitiveness of European higher education.

The EUA's next important document, the Trends-IV Report (2005), was published prior to the meeting of European higher education ministers in Bergen in 2005. The report indicated that "some scepticism" existed in certain parts of Europe towards the idea of competency-based education. The report also addressed the fact that differences regarding teaching approaches and "the degree to which student-centred learning [was a part of] [...] the everyday life at universities" prevailed (Trends-IV Report, 2005: 48). The ministers attending the 2005 Bergen meeting took note of the results and suggestions presented in the Trends-IV Report and discussed the need for continued work in the EHEA. An overarching framework for qualifications was adopted for the undergraduate, master and post-graduate levels, as well as descriptors for each cycle, "based on learning outcomes and competences" (Bergen Communiqué, 2005: 2).

In 2007, competences were briefly mentioned in the London Communiqué, in which the European higher education ministers concluded that higher education should play a strong role in "raising the level of knowledge, skills and competences in society" (London Communiqué, 2007: 5). In this Communiqué, the ministers discuss the ways in which developments have brought them "a significant step closer to the realisation of the European Higher Education Area" and mention that this area has been developed in a manner that will "facilitate mobility, increase employability and strengthen Europe's attractiveness and competitiveness".

Competences were also briefly mentioned in the Leuven/Louvain-la-Neuve Communiqué in 2009. The Communiqué, which was agreed upon in April 2009 by the ministers responsible for higher education in the then 46 countries of the Bologna Process, discussed the importance of employability and asserted that "higher education should equip students with the advanced knowledge, skills and competences they need throughout their professional lives" (Leuven/Louvain-la-Neuve Communiqué, 2009: 3).

In March 2010, the ministers of the countries participating in the Bologna Process adopted the Budapest-Vienna Declaration and officially launched the European Higher Education Area. The ministers continued to acknowledge the importance of providing students with the opportunity to acquire "knowledge, skills and competences" and agreed that the learning environment should "foster student-centred learning" (Budapest-Vienna Declaration, 2010: 2). Credit was also given to the original Bologna Declaration of 1999 and its vision for 2010, in which students would benefit from fair recognition of their qualifications.

The impact of the Bologna Process in the EHEA

Thus far, student-centred and competency-based education and students' competences on the pan-European policy level have been discussed. However, it is equally important to address these aspects from regional and national perspectives in order to fully appreciate and understand the challenges posed to teachers and staff in the institutions and departments that constitute the EHEA.

An increased pressure on higher education institutions and departments

The everyday decisions made at higher education institutions are influenced by complex issues, making it difficult to anticipate forthcoming changes and the practical implications of these changes (Newton, 2003). The Bologna Process, and the creation of the EHEA, has increased academics' workload. Moreover, increased competition between different higher education institutions to recruit students and staff has been observed. Rapid and radical changes in educational methods have also taken place as a consequence of the significant developments in computer and Internet-based education. The new type of students, who are much more familiar with utilizing the net in order to obtain information, puts new demands on the institutions of higher education in terms of innovative learning methods, such as open and distance learning, with support from information and communication technologies (ICT). These demands are coupled with an increased pressure on higher education institutions, directors and heads of departments to be accountable and to pass the audit from various authorities and governing bodies. In sum, these trends add to the overall challenges faced by educational providers who deal with issues related to teaching and learning on a daily basis in order to plan and execute high quality education and student assessments.

The lengthy introduction process: An example from Portugal

The introduction of the Bologna reform within each member state has been a lengthy process. In Portugal, for example, the implementation of the Bologna process has taken quite some time and has caused stakeholders a certain amount of trouble. One reason for these problems can be attributed to "the detailed and prescriptive traditions of the Portuguese legislation", according to Veiga & Amaral (2009: 57). In a 2006 survey of higher education institutions in Portugal, Veiga & Amaral (2009) demonstrated that universities had high expectations "of more horizontal mobility activities" at master's level after the Bologna Process was implemented. However, this expected increase in mobility has not manifested itself, partly as a result of problems with "the articulation between cycles" and "some lack of coherence between the different types of masters being developed" (Veiga & Amaral, 2009: 61). Veiga & Amaral also report issues associated with the incorrect use of the ECTS system in Portuguese higher education. Veiga & Amaral's (2009) data indicate that the priority among many institutions was to move from a teaching paradigm to a student-centred learning paradigm, stating, "Portuguese higher education institutions saw Bologna as a window of opportunity to introduce pedagogic and curricular reforms without targeting [other reforms] to the goals of Bologna" (Veiga & Amaral, 2009: 62). Veiga and Amaral concluded that the implementation of Bologna in Portugal has been "achieved in name only" (Veiga & Amaral, 2009: 67), as a consequence of the speed with which the Bologna Process was implemented and the lack of information and legislative support from the government.

The challenges of faculty development and training: An example from Spain

Díaz, Santaolalla & González (2010) conducted a study of attitudes among faculty and of the perceived training needs among these professors, to respond to the challenges of the EHEA. The study, which included 257 university teachers in humanities, social sciences, experimental sciences, health, and technology from the Complutense University of Madrid, focused on the EHEA and policy-making in general. In particular, the study focused on the knowledge and attitudes among these faculty members and the perceived training needs for the teachers based on the requirements of the EHEA. The results show that approximately one third of the teachers report that they possess only superficial knowledge about the EHEA, and approximately one third state that they are not sure how the EHEA-induced changes will affect them as teachers. 66% of the sample indicated that there is a need to change teaching methods, but at the same time 57% do not think that the structural conditions of the institution and their departments will support the development work needed to fit the education that is being offered to the requirements of the EHEA system. Based on their results, Díaz, Santaolalla & González (2010: 112) state that "faculty training causes a lot of passion to surge" and that it probably will make it even more difficult to design this type of programs.

The use of the concept of competency-based education

The term competency-based education has been contested, and certain individuals have argued that it is simply a term used by policy-makers for political and social reasons, rather than resting on a scientific basis. Hodge (2007), for example, notes that the term competency-based (or performance-based) education has been used for decades to mean different things, and claims that policy-makers in Europe currently use it as a buzzword and as a conceptual basis for redesigning curricula and learning settings within the EHEA, based on a political agenda.

Indeed, the term competency-based (or performance-based) education has long been used in various educational settings and by different organizations, such as the American Association of Colleges for Teacher Education (AACTE). For example, the AACTE appointed a Committee on Performance-Based Teacher Education in the early 1970s, which issued a list of characteristics of successful performance-based education (Elam, 1971). According to this list, competences to be demonstrated by the learner, e.g. a student, should be stated in order to be able to assess the learner's behaviour. The criteria to be used in this assessment should also be explicit and should describe the levels of competences. Moreover, the instructional programmes, that is to say, the courses, should help develop learners' competences, and the assessment of the student's competences should utilize performance as the primary source of evidence (Elam, 1971).

At least a portion of the historical roots of the concept of competency-based education lies in the USA, the Cold War era (1950-1970), and the technological competition between east and west (Hodge, 2007). The initial success of the east, with its Sputnik programme at the end of the 1950s, for example, was a thorn in the west's side and in its education and training programmes. In the USA, extensive investigations and reorganizations of schooling and professional programmes were undertaken. One result of this check-up was that the educational focus shifted from academic knowledge to practical and applicable competences and useful outcomes. Teacher education in the US was also affected by this investigation, as educational programmes were reorganised. The teacher education programmes were reformed to focus more on individual requirements and actual work requirements, and, as a consequence, changes in assessment also took place, with a stronger emphasis on evaluating performance and observable outcomes. In the late 1960s, for example, the American government issued instructions to the institutions responsible for teacher education to develop new curricula with a stronger focus on performance and behavioural outcomes, competences to be learned and the evaluation of these performances, outcomes and competences (Hodge, 2007).

Assessment and grading in the EHEA

Thus far, the concepts of student-centred and competency-based education in the EHEA have been discussed. Our attention will now turn to university teachers' evaluations of their students' competences, and towards the end we will briefly discuss grades and workplace performance after graduation.

Different assessment formats

Methods of assessing and grading undergraduate students vary across Europe (Karran, 2004, 2005; Sullivan, 2002). Numerous approaches to assessment and assessment methods testing a range of skills and abilities exist. The most common method is to let the students write exams, essays or reports, but there are many other approaches used for assessment, such as self- and peer assessment and workplace-based assessment in off-campus locations. It is important for teachers to utilise the optimal approaches and methods, based on the courses' curricula, and to give students a mix of approaches and methods, thereby enabling them to demonstrate the range of their abilities.

Traditionally, it is the teacher who assesses the students, but tutors in supervised vocational training practice or managers off-campus may also examine and grade the learning progress of students, assuming that they are prepared for this task and that they receive support. Regardless of who assesses the students, it is important that the evaluation is based on clear and available criteria and defensible evidence (Brown, 1999).

Scoring and grading students

In higher education, there are numeric scores and grades. Grades are often given in the form of letters (or some other descriptive element) and are applied to particular performances. A passing grade is often achieved when certain criteria, designed to establish whether students have reached a minimum level of competency, are met.

The grading of students, i.e. the process by which a teacher assigns values to a student's performance (for example 1-10 or A-E), plays a significant role in higher education. Grades are important to such interested parties as potential employers, Ph.D.-programme admissions committees and scholars, who analyse the effects of educational settings (Davies & Graff, 2005) or who analyse the predictive validity of grades; that is to say, to what extent grades from courses can predict future performances in graduate courses and in professional life (Gonnella, Erdmann & Hoja, 2004; Taylor & Albo, 1993). But above all, grades are important to the students themselves. Previous research confirms that students hold strong views about assessment and grading, and these views influence the ways in which students approach learning and studying (Sambell, McDowell & Brown, 1997).

Student-centred assessment

In the European Higher Education Area, assessment is regarded as something meant to enhance students' learning (Leathwood, 2005). Therefore, assessment regimes and formats are beginning to change, becoming formative rather than merely summative. In addition, the possibilities of using a variety of assessment techniques, including self- and peer assessment and problem-based learning and assessment techniques, deserve to be explored (Segers & Dochy, 2001). The problem, from the perspective of teachers who are used to multiple choice questionnaires and similar tests, is that these modern assessment forms are perceived to have lower levels of reliability and validity. Furthermore, assessment in the EHEA will also be more practical and non-academic, rather than merely scholastic and for the sole purpose of preparing undergraduates for post-graduate studies.

During the last decade, interest among educational providers in questions regarding assessment and examination has increased, as well as in how different methods of assessment affect student learning (Leathwood, 2005; Wilson & Fowler, 2005). It has become more and more common for university and college teachers to use formative assessment, rather than just summative assessment, to enhance student learning (Segers & Dochy, 2001). Formative assessment is an evaluation whose purpose entails modifying and/or improving an educational course or the students' learning environment, based on information obtained during the course. Summative assessment, on the other hand, refers to the traditional method of assessing students; it takes place at the conclusion of a course, with the purpose of determining the course's effectiveness and the students' grades (Roos, 2005).

The relationship between grades and future workplace success

Research focusing on grades and workplace performance after graduation makes use of two theories: cognitive skills theory claims that students develop their cognitive skills during their time at university and that their levels of performance are visible in their grades. These achievements then lead to success in the workplace, and, since productivity is rewarded with increased earnings, "a positive relationship should exist between academic achievement and earnings" (Donhardt, 2004: 281), as "the more educated the employee, the more productive he/she is [...] and that employers reward more highly educated workers with higher pay" (Donhardt, 2004: 273). Meanwhile, certification theory claims that job applicants' certificates (degrees and diplomas) are what matters to employers, rather than grades. According to this theory, grades have no influence on future earnings.

Donhardt (2004) studied earnings' outcomes by exploring the prediction and growth of earnings over the first 3 years following graduation. Grades were the measure of academic accomplishment, and earnings were indicative of the value ascribed to an individual. Donhardt wished to determine whether achievement in college, as measured by grade point average, can predict the growth of earnings over time. He expected "grade point average to be key in the relationship" (Donhardt, 2004: 281). Nevertheless, his results indicated that grade point average had little impact on earnings. GPA was not a significant variable and had very little correlation with earnings. Nor did students with high grades experience significantly higher growth of earnings over time when compared with students with lower grades. Donhardt concluded the certification theory, which claims that job applicants are often screened based on their university degrees, since degree certificates designate the student as a hard worker, to be more plausible. This finding is nothing new to researchers in higher education. In previous research, Pascarella & Terenzini (1991), for example, have demonstrated that a positive association exists between having a college or university degree and success in the workplace.

Looking ahead

The most recent Ministerial Meeting was hosted by Romania in Bucharest on April 26-27, 2012. At this meeting, the ministers investigated the progress that had been made in the Leuven/Louvain-la-Neuve agenda and expressed their continued strife to drive it forward. The following ministerial conferences will be held in 2015, 2018 and 2020. What can be expected in the near future with respect to higher education in Europe? Competency-based education and student-centred assessment methodologies will most certainly continue to be utilized, just as the merchandisation of higher education seems likely to continue. Global economic factors will continue to influence educational systems and the labour markets, and higher education institutions will face even fiercer economic competition from one another.

This paper has described the general agreements and the international character of the Bologna Process; the various actors and organisations involved have only been superficially outlined. Many more structures and factors impact the Bologna Process and affect the EHEA. For the institutions and departments, it is vital to be conscious of structures and factors at the local level; for example, in the planning and implementation of professional development and training for university teachers and other staff. In these efforts, it is important to acknowledge, for example, "the teachers' own needs, the possible differences associated to scientific scopes, and academic and age category", as Díaz, Santaolalla & González (2010: 117) remind us.

Bibliography

Adam, S. (2001). A pan-European credit accumulation framework: Dream or disaster? *Higher Education Quarterly, 55*(3), 292-305.

Bergen Communiqué (2005). *The European Higher Education Area: Achieving the Goals Communiqué of the Conference of European Ministers Responsible for Higher Education.* 19-20 May. Bergen.

Berlin Communiqué. (2003). *Realising the European Higher Education Area: Communiqué of the Conference of Ministers Responsible for Higher Education.* 19 September. Berlin.

Bologna Declaration (1999). *Joint Declaration of the European Ministers of Education.* 19 June. Bologna.

Brown, S. (1999). Institutional strategies for assessment. In S. Brown & A. Glasner (Eds.), *Assessment Matters in Higher Education: Choosing and Using Diverse Approaches* (pp. 3-13). Maidenhead: Open University Press.

Budapest-Vienna Declaration (2010). *Budapest-Vienna Declaration on the European Higher Education Area.* March 12. Budapest-Vienna.

Davies, J., & Graff, M. (2005). Performance in e-learning: Online participation and student grades. *British Journal of Educational Technology, 36*(4), 657-663.

Díaz, M. J. F., Santaolalla, R. C., & González, A. G. (2010). Faculty attitudes and training needs to respond the new European Higher Education challenges. *Higher Education, 60*(1), 101-118.

Donhardt, G. L. (2004). In search of the effects of academic achievement in postgraduate earnings. *Research in Higher Education, 45*(3), 271-284.

Elam, S. (1971). *Performance-based Teacher Education. What is the State of the Art?* Washington: American Association of Colleges for Teacher Education.

European University Association (2005). *Trends IV: European Universities Implementing Bologna*. Brussels: EUA.

Gonnella, J. S., Erdmann, J. B., & Hoja, M. (2004). An empirical study of the predictive validity of number grades in medical school using 3 decades of longitudinal data: Implications for a grading system. *Medical Education, 38*(4), 425-434.

Graz Declaration. (2003). *Forward from Berlin: The Role of the Universities*. 28-30 May. Graz.

Heinze, T., & Knill, C. (2008). Analysing the differential impact of the Bologna Process: Theoretical considerations on national conditions for international policy convergence. *Higher Education, 56*(4), 493-510.

Hodge, S. (2007). The origins of competency-based training. *Australian Journal of Adult Learning, 47*(2), 179-209.

Karran, T. (2004). Achieving Bologna convergence: Is ECTS failing to make the grade? *Higher Education in Europe, 24*(3), 411-421.

Karran, T. (2005). Pan-European grading scales: Lessons from national systems and the ECTS. *Higher Education in Europe, 30*(1), 5-22.

Leathwood, C. (2005). Assessment policy and practice in higher education: Purpose, standards and equity. *Assessment & Evaluation in Higher Education, 30*(3), 307-324.

Leuven and Louvain-la-Neuve Communiqué. (2009). *The Bologna Process 2020: The European Higher Education Area in the New Decade. Communiqué of the Conference of European Ministers Responsible for Higher Education*. 28-29 April. Leuven and Louvain-la-Neuve.

Lisbon Recognition Convention (1997). *Council of Europe/UNESCO Convention on the Recognition of Qualifications Concerning Higher Education in the European Region*. 11 April. Lisbon.

London Communiqué. (2007). *Towards the European Higher Education Area: Responding to Challenges in a Globalised World.* 18 May. London.

NCIHE (1997). *Higher Education in the Learning Society: A Summary Report*. London: Her Majesty's Stationery Office (HMSO).

Newton, J. (2003). Implementing an institution-wide learning and teaching strategy: Lessons in managing change. *Studies in Higher Education, 28*(4), 427-441.

Otter, S. (1993). Learning outcomes in higher education. In J. Burke (Ed.), *Outcomes, Learning and the Curriculum: Implications for NVQ's, GNVQ's and Qualifications* (pp. 273-284). London: Routledge.

Pascarella, E. T., & Terenzini, P. T. (1991). *How College Affects Students. Findings and Insights from Twenty Years of Research*. San Francisco: Jossey-Bass Publishers.

Prague Communiqué (2001). *Towards the European Higher Education Area: Communiqué of the Meeting of European Ministers in Charge of Higher Education.* 19 May. Prague.

Roos, B. (2005). *ICT and Formative Assessment in the Learning Society* [Academic Diss.]. Umeå: Umeå University, Department of Education.

Sambell, K., McDowell, L., & Brown, S. (1997). "But is it fair?": An exploratory study of student perceptions of the consequential validity of assessment. *Studies in Educational Evaluation, 23*(4), 349-371.

Segers, M., & Dochy, F. (2001). New assessment forms in problem-based learning: The value-added of the students' perspective. *Studies in Higher Education, 26*(3), 327-343.

Sorbonne Declaration (1998). *Joint Declaration on Harmonisation of the Architecture of the European Higher Education System by the Four Ministers in Charge for France, Germany, Italy and the United Kingdom.* 25 May. Paris.

Sullivan, K. (2002). Credit and grade transfer within the European Union's SOCRATES Programme: Unity in diversity or head in the sand? *Assessment & Evaluation in Higher Education, 27*(1), 65-74.

Taylor, C. W., & Albo, D. (1993). Measuring and predicting the performances of practising physicians: An overview of two decades of research at the University of Utah. *Academic Medicine, 68*(2), 65-67.

Tuning (2006). *Tuning Educational Structures in Europe. General Brochure.* Retrieved from http://unideusto.org/tuningeu (01/01/2013).

Veiga, A., & Amaral, A. (2009). Survey on the implementation of the Bologna Process in Portugal. *Higher Education, 57*(1), 57-69.

Wilson, K., & Fowler, J. (2005). Assessing the impact of learning environments on students' approaches to learning: Comparing conventional and action learning designs. *Assessment & Evaluation in Higher Education, 30*(1), 87-101.

Foreign Language Teaching in Europe

Edited by:
Manuel Jiménez Raya, Terry Lamb and Flávia Viera

Vol. 1 Pamela Faber / Wolf Gewehr / Manuel Jiménez Raya / Antony Peck (Eds.): English Teacher Education in Europe. New Trends and Developments. 1999.

Vol. 2 Stephan H. Gabel: Über- und Unterrepräsentation im Lernerenglisch. Untersuchungen zum Sprachgebrauch deutscher Schülerinnen und Schüler in interkulturellen Telekommunikationsprojekten. 2000.

Vol. 3 Winfried Bredenbröker: Förderung der fremdsprachlichen Kompetenz durch bilingualen Unterricht. Empirische Untersuchungen. 2000.

Vol. 4 Manuel Jiménez Raya / Pamela Faber / Wolf Gewehr / Antony J. Peck (eds.): Effective Foreign Language Teaching at the Primary Level. 2001.

Vol. 5 Yvette Coyle / Mercedes Verdú / Marisol Valcárcel: Teaching English to Children - Interactivity and Teaching Strategies in the Primary FL Classroom. 2002.

Vol. 6 Markus Kötter: Tandem learning on the Internet. Learner interactions in virtual online environments (MOOs). 2002.

Vol. 7 Manuel Jiménez Raya / Terry Lamb (eds.): Differentiation in the Modern Languages Classroom. 2003.

Vol. 8 Kees van Esch / Oliver St. John (eds.): A Framework for Freedom. Learner Autonomy in Foreign Language Teacher Education. 2003.

Vol. 9 Kees van Esch / Oliver St. John (eds.): New Insights into Foreign Language Learning and Teaching. 2004.

Vol. 10 Manuel Jiménez Raya / Lies Sercu (eds.): Challenges in Teacher Development: Learner Autonomy and Intercultural Competence. 2007.

Vol. 11 Flávia Vieira (ed.): Struggling for Autonomy in Language Education. Reflecting, Acting, and Being. 2009.

Vol. 12 María Luisa Pérez Cañado / Juan Ráez Padilla (eds.): Digital Competence Development in Higher Education. An International Perspective. 2014.

www.peterlang.com

www.ingramcontent.com/pod-product-compliance
Ingram Content Group UK Ltd.
Pitfield, Milton Keynes, MK11 3LW, UK
UKHW041827031026
15587UKWH00002B/609

9 783631 638033